D1615297

3 4130 00002209 0

AVENGER FROM THE SKY

Avenger from the Sky

Donald Judd

WILLIAM KIMBER · LONDON

First published in 1985 by
WILLIAM KIMBER & CO. LIMITED
100 Jermyn Street, London, SW1Y 6EE

© Donald Judd, 1985
ISBN 0-7183-0568-X

70 22

Photoset by
Print Co-ordination, Macclesfield, Cheshire
and printed in Great Britain by
Redwood Burn Limited, Trowbridge.

To
my wife Jean
with love

Contents

List of Illustrations

All photographs are from the author's collection

LIST OF MAPS

Preface

This book is not intended to be a history of anything. Nor is it a commentary on the times or the period covered by World War II. It simply recounts my experiences in those, for me, bitter sweet years as a dive-bomber, as it turned out, with the Fleet Air Arm. The only documentary evidence that I have used was my log books written up faithfully after every flight, together with the notes that I would add, quite illegally, I am sure, of anything pertinent or unusual in the flight, operation or the situation generally. Of course, memory plays a part, and although it is now over 40 years old, many will agree with me that very often an incident that took place in those five years is as vivid as if it took place yesterday. But my log books were the only real source of the tale that I have tried to relate. Nothing takes the place of facts or impressions written down at the time and I have leaned heavily on them for the contents of this book.

D.J.

CHAPTER ONE

Prelude

The day began as one of those ordinary days; that is, if you can call any day in Egypt in 1941 ordinary. In any case, I was in no position at that time to describe a day in Egypt since I had arrived there from England only some two weeks before at the beginning of July 1941. I had, however, been there long enough to realise that this was a different world from that which I had known in England.

Here in Egypt, it was soon evident that there were two widely divergent classes of people, the extremely wealthy and the very poor, the privileged, the slaves, the bosses and the beggars and not much in between. The wealthy upper class were few while the beggars and the touts accosted the passer-by at every street corner. The air was heavy, hot and humid, the smell of garlic rife, the sun beat down day after day and the flies were everywhere and in their element whether feeding on a beggar's sore or on food. It was filthy, sweaty, certainly corrupt and impossibly slow and indolent. But these very characteristics made it fascinating and interesting. It had a mystery about it, common to the whole of the Eastern Mediterranean. Something perhaps to do with the history of the area. It was indeed a change from the country of my upbringing.

I was part of a draft of some dozen or so Fleet Air Arm pilots and observers sent out as newly trained aircrew ostensibly to relieve the old timers on the carriers in the Eastern Mediterranean fleet. We looked upon ourselves as something in our new sub-lieutenant's uniform and complete with wings and 200 hours flying including a practice deck landing or two under our belts. This feeling was soon to be dashed when it was brought home to us that we were just sprogs newly out of training, a fact that was often rammed down our throats by the experienced aircrew with whom we now came into contact. We had to earn the wings that had been given to us. We had disembarked from the SS *Georgic*, one of White Star Line's cruise ships, at Suez and shepherded by train through Cairo to Alexandria and then to HMS Grebe, the naval name given to the Fleet Air Arm's base airfield some few miles west of Alexandria. Dekheila was its local name; before the war it had been Alexandria's civil airport. We were assigned to the squadron, No 775, attached to the base until Their Lordships had decided how best to employ us on more lethal pursuits.

Dekheila was a pleasant and well equipped airfield with concrete runways, plenty of hangar space and a spacious and airy mess. It was well established and well run. But we soon found out that there was no carrier to which we could be posted. HMS *Illustrious* had been badly damaged on the way to and in Malta in January 1941 and had to stagger to the United States for massive repairs. HMS *Formidable* came out from the UK round the Cape and had taken the place of *Illustrious,* but after sterling work in the Greek and Crete campaigns, had been badly damaged off Crete on 16th May 1941 after an attack on Scarpanto airfield. When we arrived in Alex, she was lying damaged at her moorings in the harbour waiting to follow *Illustrious* to the United States to be repaired. The *Formidable's* air squadrons had been disembarked to Dekheila. The temporary loss of these two carriers together with the immense losses suffered by the three Services in their vain attempt to hold the Germans in Greece and then in Crete had its effect on morale in Egypt. Then there was Rommel's arrival in Libya with his much vaunted Afrika Korps earlier in the year followed by his recapture of all the ground gained by Wavell in 1940 except for Tobruk. It looked like a strong pincer movement by Hitler to grab the Middle East and secure the oil supplies of the area as far away as the Persian Gulf.

There was a prevailing air of gloom around the place. Experienced front line squadrons and their aircrews were lolling around with nowhere to go and nothing to do; replacements wondered why they were there at all. It has often been said with much truth that the life of a wartime pilot was divided into two sides – half the time he ws shit-scared and the other half, bored bloody stiff. These first few weeks were some of the many examples of the latter.

But, as Bernard Shaw once said, 'You never can tell'. On this particular day, I was in the crewroom of 775 Squadron doing nothing better than reading the *Egyptian Mail* when someone called my name and added, 'Someone wants to see you in 826 Squadron – the senior pilot, I think'.

'What the hell does he want?'

'How should I know – better get over there.'

I grabbed my cap and made my way to the next hangar which housed 826 Squadron. One of the offices in the corner was marked 'Senior Pilot – Lieut. Abrams RN'. Taking a deep breath and tucking my cap underneath my left arm, naval style, I knocked on the door.

'Come in,' said a voice from inside.

Before I could close the door, Abrams from behind his desk said, 'Oh! Judd, would you like a suicide job?'

Fortunately, I didn't have to give a silly answer to an impossible question as he went on, 'I am leaving the squadron and we need a new pilot. Go and get your things and report to the crewroom – someone will look after you there.'

I retired with mixed feelings of apprehension and hopeful expectation, but overall very glad to have a posting to a squadron wherever that would take me.

No 826 Squadron was already famous. It had been formed at Ford in Sussex in 1940 and started its long operational career (which still continues after two or three recommissionings) at Bircham Newton in Norfolk. It had spent the rest of that year carrying out dive bombing and minelaying operations in the new 100 mph Albacore along the Dutch, Belgian and French coasts. At the end of the year it joined HMS *Formidable* bound for the Eastern Mediterranean. Attacks were carried out along the Red Sea Coast. In the Mediterranean, based at Alex, the squadron flew many successful operations off *Formidable* including the attack on the Italian Fleet in the Battle of Cape Matapan before *Formidable* was put out of action off Crete.

So, I was brought down to earth when I realised that I was to be a new boy among such élite. And it was with a daunting feeling in my stomach that I arrived at the 826 crewroom. My reception didn't help, either. All flying crewrooms have the same atmosphere especially when there is no flying on. They resemble a cross between a cricket club changing room on a wet day and what I imagine a

Chicago gunman's hideout was like when there was only time to kill and nothing in prospect. Everyone has his own pitch on the wall bench and woebetide anyone who trespasses. There will be a poker school in the corner where the accusations of cheating and swearing are rife. Others will have their feet up reading pornographic literature; the more serious of those present will, however, be deep into more classical literature like James Hadley Chase. Some who beat it up the night before will be nodding off to sleep, while almost certainly the eager-beaver will be doing something constructive like checking up on the silhouettes of enemy aircraft. No intelligent sounds can be heard other than the odd swear-word aimed probably at the non-present CO or the system in general but the air will somehow be full of inactivity and smoke and the whole place looks like a shambles. The centre table will be full of parachute packs, Mae Wests, helmets and other flying clothing. The floor will be covered with the same sort of items. Dirty magazines and books will be scattered around. The walls will be covered with all sorts of photographs. Perhaps a sheet containing pictures of all enemy aircraft, a map of the area, a notice board with irrelevant information on it jostling for position with Lana Turner, Betty Grable and Mae West herself, in various states of undress. It is a sanctuary where no unauthorized person is allowed to enter.

As I entered, there was barely a movement. A member of the poker school looked up, grunted and then returned to guard his cards and money. Someone glanced up from the *Razzle* that he was reading but took no further interest. I refrained from saying anything but was saved by a kindly soul who came over –

'You're the new pilot.'

'Yes.'

'What's your name?'

'Judd.'

Thus started one of the memorable years of my life.

CHAPTER TWO

Beginnings

I suppose it all started back in 1930 or 1931. As a twelve-year-old, I had been fascinated, like all my contemporaries, with the new phenomenon of flying. I had avidly read all about the great aces of World War 1 like Ball, McCudden and Richthofen with their Sopwiths and Fokkers. Imperial Airways had caught my imagination with their flights to Paris and other places in Europe in what looked like vast machines such as the Handley Page Hannibal – with their luxury service. Croydon airport was their English base and the mecca of all aircraft enthusiasts together with Hendon and its annual flying display. Then there was the famous race to Australia in 1934 won by the British plane, a Comet DH88. I had my ears glued to the wireless to catch every move and my knowledge of world geography increased with news of landings at Aleppo, Karachi and all places East. Then my imagination was caught by the pre-World War II generation of the great Hawker Military aircraft such as the Fury, Hart (little did I then know that I would be flying one of them), the Audax and the Nimrod.

One day I spotted in the local paper that Alan Cobham was bringing his Air Show to my home town, Guildford, in two or three weeks. The notice went on to say that on a Saturday before the show, a plane would be flying over the town and the first twelve to guess its height correctly would qualify for a free flight. On the day, I came near enough to guessing the height of the plane to earn me the coveted prize. Off I went to the show to see the aerobatics and all the famous planes. Then came the moment I had been waiting for to climb into the De Havilland for the long awaited flight. Above the sprawling mass of humanity and over my home and all the country I knew so well, it brought to reality all the pictures of aircraft that I had collected. It was without a doubt one of the great experiences of my youth; the flying bug had entered the system where it has firmly remained ever since.

But life went on at school; then I was articled to the Town Clerk of Guildford at the same time, attending University College, London to study for a Law Degree. However, the dark clouds were rolling over Europe and 1938 brought Munich and war looked inevitable. Although I was lucky enough to graduate in June 1939, I realised that I would be involved in any conflict. I wanted to join the Navy but the flying bug had got hold of me. How could I combine the two?

By October 1939 the Navy was over-subscribed. However, I went to the Admiralty to see if there was any hope, to be told that the only way of getting to sea was by joining the Fleet Air Arm. So, I spent a month or so fitting in my Solicitors Finals exam, (after all, the war wouldn't last that long!), meantime applying to join the Fleet Air Arm. I was accepted though subject to a medical examination. I did not fear the medical as such, as rugby, cricket and squash had kept me pretty fit. However, the close-work of studying for exams for three years had forced me to take to glasses for reading. I decided, after much worrying, to leave the glasses behind when I was called to the medical at Portsmouth. There were no problems in the event and that was the end of specs for many years to come. I was accepted and told to report to HMS St Vincent, a shore-based establishment at Gosport, on 1st April 1940.

It was ironic that I joined the FAA to get to sea, yet I did not join a naval ship until over three years later. However, meantime I got all the flying hours I wanted.

My first brush with naval establishment came in an immediate and unexpected way. In the middle of March I got German measles. Clearly I would not be able to join His Majesty's Navy on the due date so my mother sent off a telegram to HMS St Vincent roughly in the following terms 'Regret my son Donald Judd will not be able to join up on 1st April owing to his having contracted German measles. He will report when fit.'

I thought nothing of it and when discharged by the doctor, I packed my bag and made my way to Gosport. My heart sank when I approached St Vincent. Its grey square block and barrack ground looked more like a prison than a 'ship' of the Navy. Had I come to the right place, and if I had, had I done the right thing in volunteering for this? What a hell of a hole. However, worse was to come. The rating on the gate confirmed that it was indeed HMS St Vincent and directed me to a hut beyond the square and told me to report to the officer in charge.

I knocked and entered what appeared to be the appropriate door to see a Lieutenant-Commander standing at his desk.

'Judd, sir, Donald Judd reporting for duty, sir.'

That did it. The face got redder, aggressive and angry. His stature seemed to expand like a balloon to near bursting point. He obviously thought that he had a skiver on his hands.

'What the hell are you doing reporting two weeks late. You're absent without leave.'

'Oh, sir, didn't you get my Mother's telegram? I've had German measles' said I naively.

'I couldn't care less what you've had. I've a good mind to report you to the Captain.'

'Yes, sir,' I said.

He continued the diatribe but soon he began running out of steam. And with a further 'Don't let it happen again' I was dismissed, as if joining up in the Navy was a weekly occurrence! Not at all a good beginning, I thought, as I left his office feeling more like a criminal than a budding naval officer, and for the second time within the hour, wondering whether I was doing the right thing.

But things improved. I was kitted out in bell bottoms as an ordinary seaman. The only difference from the normal rating's uniform was that the hat band was marked 'FLEET AIR ARM' and we wore a white band on our left sleeve to indicate that we were officer cadets. There was some question as to whether it was legal to have a hat band so marked. The normal hat band in war time just had HMS on it. No name of the ship for security purposes. So we had two bands which we changed outside the gates of the establishment. I joined No 13 course, some 70 strong. We ratings occupied large dormitories and one mess hall. The course was to last nearly two months and the general idea of it was to teach us naval ways and to knock a bit of discipline into us. I don't think that either plan succeeded, much as the resident course officers and petty officers did their best. But it was clear from the start that they were fighting a losing battle and they knew it, judging by the look of despair that constantly crossed their faces.

We had lectures in knots and splicing, morse, map-reading, the history and organization of the Navy, warships and their uses and the eternal square bashing. Half of us had opted to be pilots, the other half observers and we all wondered what all this had to do with flying, a word that was hardly used in such a basic naval establishment. We could not wait until the end of May to start the real thing.

When kitted out, the first exercise was to learn to make one's bed (or rather unmake it) in the mornings all ship-shape and naval fashion. Inspections were often made, so there was no getting away with it. And then on with the course on a strict timetable basis. In spite of the frustrations, it was a happy course – the more bull there was, the more laughter. The members of the course came from all over the country, many from universities; most were characters and all had a sense of humour. That was essential for survival. It was hard to think that Hitler's forces were getting near our doorstep and that the invasion of England was being talked about. The only thing in our minds was the end of the course.

Apart from my introduction to the place, I can now only remember two specific incidents at HMS St Vincent.

One was the first pay parade. I don't know why it has stuck in my mind except perhaps because it was the first money I had earned. Solicitors' Articled Clerks (or rather their fathers) had to pay a capital sum for the privilege of being articled in those days and there was no question of repayment or any other payment being made to the Clerk by his Principal. We paraded in the open air in front of the Paymaster standing behind a desk with his Petty Officer. Before arriving at his desk, the order was given 'off caps'. The hand was crossed to the rim and cap held flat top upwards in front of the chest, like Oliver Twist asking for more. On the name being checked and the amount stated the cash was placed loose on the hat. You then covered the money with your left hand and doubled back to your place in the ranks. I think my first week's pay was three shillings and sixpence. I remember making a mental note that this would buy me several pints of beer, fags and food to augment the drab fare at Vincent. I thought that this was a great day. It was to be repeated 44 years later with different money and in different circumstances but with the same unaccountable excitement when I formed up in the queue at the local Post Office to collect my first week's National Insurance Pension.

The other incident concerned our 'Sergeant-Major', Petty Officer Oliver. He was a memorable man and I guarantee that everyone of the hundreds who went through Vincent will remember him with a mixture of awe, fear, dread and affection. I shall never know how he kept his cool (sufficiently to keep within naval regulations) in the face of the unruly, rebellious, humorous platoons which it was his unenviable duty to try and discipline. Any lesser man would have collapsed beneath the frustration of it. He had a voice that could be heard in Portsmouth Dockyard, eyes all the way round his head that could pick up the slightest blemish in dress or mistake in drill, ears that would detect the whispered word among the ranks, a wit that was as quick and cutting as any can be, and a sarcasm that would make the toughest recruit shiver.

One day we were doing bayonet drill. One of the moves in unfixing bayonets took the bayonet across the body to be held just above the scabbard and kept in place by the left hand. On the appropriate order the bayonet was pushed home hard provided it didn't cut off the fingers of the left hand in the process. All carried out the order except one of the platoon, poor Ordinary Seaman Gaze, who fiddled with the point of the bayonet without being able to house it in the scabbard. As quick as a flash, PO Oliver bawled, 'Gize, 'avin a little bit of trouble?' 'Yes, sir.' 'Can't find the 'ole eh?' 'No, sir.' Then with a voice more powerful and strident – 'So, Gize, what 'appens when ...' But the rest was drowned as the platoon fell about with laughter, but not for long, before the iron hand of PO Oliver came down. 'The platoon will double march round the parade ground twice. Left turn, double march. Left, right, left, right ...' And we were not that fit but there was no stopping him until two circuits were achieved and the laughter had long since disappeared from our faces. That was followed by a lecture vaguely on the thesis of naval discipline by Petty Officer Oliver, interspersed with sarcasm and all the swear words in the book.

It was not all black however. 'Shore' leave was allowed every evening and this invariably meant a run 'ashore' over the ferry to Portsmouth to sample the local pubs and the beer at 6d (old money) per pint. These runs 'ashore' meant a rowdy and drunken return to the dormitory to the annoyance of those who had chosen to have an early night.

On one of these trips ashore, a group of us were in a pub near the Guildhall. The bar was packed, loud and smoky with beer being sloshed all over the place as pints were passed back to those furthest from the bar. Suddenly the door opened and an RN Commander walked in with a girl and made straight for the stairs. This was so obviously not cricket that a hush came over the occupants of the bar, a fact recognised by the landlord simultaneously. The landlord boomed out, 'You can't go up there, sir', at which the Commander and his companion beat a hasty retreat through the door to the cheers of the drinkers mixed with a certain amount of sympathy for the Commander and his missed opportunity.

And weekend leave was given half way through the course which was a good chance to taste home made cooking again – a relief from the mass produced mince and two underdone veg and Nelson Tart.

CHAPTER 3

Learning to Fly

None of us were sorry when the first part of our training came to an end and no tears were shed when we finally walked out through the gates of HMS St Vincent.

The course divided at this point. The future observers went off to their new course while the pilots were posted to No 14 Elementary Flying Training School at Elmdon, Birmingham. There were thirty of us to be joined by five RN and RNR Officers. Elmdon had been and still is Birmingham's airport, then a grass airfield with a small (by modern standards) airport terminal where the course offices were and where we lived and slept. We were to be there for six weeks, doing the elementary flying training in Tiger Moths. All the instructors except one RN officer, and all the maintenance personnel were RAF.

The history of military flying in England must be appreciated in this context. In the First World War, military flying was divided between the Navy with its Royal Naval Air Service, and the Army under the Royal Flying Corps. Towards the end of the war the Royal Air Force was founded to combine the two air services and to take over all military flying in Britain. The RNAS to all intents and purposes ceased to exist until, after a long struggle, the Navy got back control of naval aviation in 1937. However, there was a problem with personnel since the Navy did not have the trained groundcrew to take over from the RAF. Naval pilots and observers were trained with the help of the new Short Service Commissions designated RN(A) or A Boys. These were followed by the Royal Naval Volunteer Reserve Flyers who were joining from 1939 onwards in ever increasing numbers. But at Elmdon for example, all the groundcrew were RAF and in many naval squadrons, particularly those that were shore-based, the NCO's were RAF personnel until as late as 1943.

My instructor was Flying Officer Walls, said to be the son of Tom Walls and in appearance not unlike David Niven. There was however, no light-hearted approach to flying; it was very stern stuff indeed, not surprisingly when we consider that the instructor was putting himself in the hands of someone who hadn't flown before – a fact that was only too self-evident during most of the course and especially before 'going solo'. We were given the strictest instructions before any flying commenced as to procedure and particularly the relationship between instructor and pupil. It was of course essential that the instructor be able to take over in a split second if the pupil had the controls and things were going wrong. The instructor would call down the voice pipe, 'I've got her'. Then the pupil took hands and feet off the controls and quick. There could be no room for any misunderstanding. It was not unknown for a pupil to 'freeze' on the controls through sheer fright which could be disastrous. So, the instructor had to act quickly, in time but without shouting or panic. Flying Officer Walls was an excellent instructor from the pupils' point of view. He said little but always spoke concisely, precisely, leaving no room for doubt. There was no chat or small talk in the air. It was a serious business indeed.

The Tiger Moth is, in my mind, one of the great planes of all time. It had perfect aerodynamics and was as safe as houses provided it was properly flown. It had to be flown and seemed to cry out for perfect treatment. It was a joy to fly if handled correctly but soon became bolshy if there was the slightest hint of the ham-fisted approach. The gliding, as opposed to the powered approach, called for precision flying. A knot or two under the correct speed, according to wind conditions and it would fall out of the sky; a knot or two over and in pulling back the stick to achieve the three point landing, it would balloon into the air, both with potentially disastrous results. The perfect three point landing without hitting the ground and ballooning was very difficult to achieve. It was a knack but one which took a long time to master. When you got it, it was a delight to experience.

The Elementary Flying Course to me, more than the rest of the flying course, was a mixture of emotions. The sheer joy of experiencing for the first time flying at the controls of a plane above the hurly burly of the world, the freedom of being in the sky in complete charge, provided the propeller kept going round, was something that is quite indescribable. It is like nothing else I know. This sensation got into my blood during those six weeks and has never dissolved. It cannot be explained, only experienced.

But the course was intense and to a large degree traumatic. Would one make the first solo, and if so, would one be able to complete the course? EFTS was a case of many being called, but fewer chosen. A number couldn't go solo in the requisite time allotted; some were not cut out for flying; some were psychologically unfit to fly; and some were just plain air-sick.

The first solo is perhaps one of the most unforgettable experiences of life. You get more and more tensed-up as the magical ten hours' flying time approaches. You get little encouragement from your instructor; the only thing you know is that you haven't been slung out yet like others in the course. The regularity with which this took place in the early stages was distinctly unnerving. You suddenly have an inkling that 'the day' might be imminent as your instructor concentrates a flying session on take-offs and landings. Then you are told to stay in the cockpit while the Chief Flying Instructor comes out and climbs in to give you an independent check-out.

This time it is 50 minutes of take-offs and landings. Not a hint from the CFI that you are doing well or badly, other than a good many criticisms. Yet another landing and are you going to be told to pack your bags?

Then suddenly, after you've come to a halt, near Flying Control, the CFI undoes his straps, climbs down the wing, leaning over your cockpit and shouts, 'It's all yours.' 'It's all mine?' It must be rather like the condemned man being told, 'Come on – this is it.' You can't get out of the plane and say to your instructor 'Please, sir, not today; I don't feel like it.' You just have to grin and bear it. It is inevitable and it has to be done. There is no way out, no escape. The world stands still, the mind freezes. It seems that you are now on show, and all eyes are upon you.

Something tells you, 'Don't just sit there, do something' and you do. You start to rev up, turn round and make for the down wind edge of the field. You half turn into wind, do your checks, see that no plane is coming into land, or taking off. You realise suddenly that there is not the comforting head in the cockpit in front of you. You are alone, completely and utterly. You automatically turn into wind and open up the throttle. You are numb but you hope for the best. You get into the air. Well, that wasn't too bad. Didn't dig the nose in the ground, didn't swing, got off the deck. But, dear Lord, I've got to get down again in one piece and no instructor to take over if I am making a balls of it. Your fears begin to evaporate as you climb, level off and turn left and left again to fly down wind. Good, there's the airfield; better turn across wind; that and the next turn into the wind are the vital ones. Well, it looks all right. Better get into the glide. Am I flying her or is she flying me? I don't know, but we are over the fence at the right height. Well done, old girl, you really didn't need me, did you?

Suddenly as you come to a stop, elation and a cold sweat breaks out. You shout above the slipstream, 'Whoopee, I've made it on my own.'

You taxi in to the hangar apron, turn off the engine and get out when the chocks have been placed in front of the wheels. There's your instructor waiting. You would think he would be over the moon. But there isn't a change of expression. All he says is, 'That was OK. Report here at 2.30.' That afternoon which you could well use sleeping off the emotion, is spent with more landing practice, spinning and climbing turns, followed by your second solo flight. This, if anything, is rather worse than the first. A little knowledge is ...

You get pissed that evening.

But this opens up a lot of new vistas to you. You can get away on your own to do some loops and rolls and spins. It was a joy flying in and out of white clouds, shooting them up and gliding down them until you realised that the instructor had set you specific manoeuvres to practise, so they had to be fitted in before your time was up. I remember one lovely Sunday morning, finding the Golf Course near Hampden-in-Arden. It was full of desperately serious foursomes. What an opportunity to show off. So I picked a long fairway and flew low up it to the green. The anger of the golfers was obvious enough. 'I say, George, haven't those young hooligans any discipline these days. I know there's a war on, but ...' could I hear them say? But it didn't dampen my joy. No wonder the CO got a few complaints from the Secretary.

In between, were lectures on navigation and map reading, the theory of flight, aerodynamics, the working of an internal combusion engine. They were made very interesting and we all took them seriously as we knew there was to be an exam at the end of the course. That wasn't too difficult. I don't remember anyone failing it.

One strange general impression that I carried away from this course was the total lack of impact that the war had on us and our life at Elmdon, bearing in mind that while we were there, the Germans reached the Channel coast, Dunkirk took place and Paris fell. We might have been training in the middle of peacetime in this gloriously hot and sunny summer of 1940. The only hint of war was when we were informed that there would be a visit by some top brass to look at the feasibility of fitting bomb racks to the wings of the Tiger Moths so that the pupils could bomb the Germans on the beaches in the event of an invasion. Churchill's exhortation that, 'We shall fight on the beaches, we shall fight on the landing-grounds ...', came awfully near home. Fortunately we were never called upon to make this warlike effort.

And we had our fun too. We had a free half day every week. One of our number was a local cricketer and he arranged games with village teams in the district. Of course, we were always in uniform – bell-bottoms – and one evening coming back from a match at Solihull and feeling thirsty, we stopped the van at a likely looking pub. Twelve of us filed into the pub where there were three or four locals at the bar. 'Pints all round for the tars, landlord,' said one, before we reached the bar. Another local followed this with a further round and so on. We did our best to return the hospitality but to no avail. We were not allowed to buy a drink.

The same thing happened when we went into Birmingham for a meal. Sometimes during the meal, an old lady would tap one of us on the shoulder. 'It is all paid for, Jack,' or when we went to the cash desk to pay, we would be told that another customer had already paid for everything.

What a welcome we were given in and around Birmingham.

We then moved to No 7 Service Flying Training School at Peterborough on 20th July 1940. I had flown 35 hours dual in Tiger Moths and 28 hours on my own. We were to be at Peterborough for six weeks. Again, although the war was getting closer with the Battle of Britain in full swing, we had no experience of it nor did it interfere with our training. It might have been peacetime and still the long hot summer continued.

The course was more service-orientated than the Elementary Course at Elmdon. Peterborough was an old and well-established RAF aerodrome. Not that we did much flying from the airfield itself; we flew and did our training at a large grass field at Sibsen on the other side of the Great North Road. The planes were flown over to Sibsen by the instructors and some pupils in the morning, the rest of us following in buses with such groundcrew as was required. We then returned after the last flight in the afternoon. While we continued with the usual take-off and landings, turns, aerobatics, spinning, we had more instrument flying practice, more navigation and cross country flying and the beginnings of night flying. This was clearly the start of the serious flying, a conversion course on to the Hawker Hart. It was made of sterner stuff than the Tiger Moth. An ex-RAF operational plane, it not only sounded powerful, but, for those days, was powerful. No hand-swinging of the propeller to start the engine, but an automatic cockpit starter. The engine was powerful and it was a super plane to fly in every respect. It had a deep-throated roar to it and was quick to answer to throttle. The surge in take-off was positive and something that was unknown in the Tiger Moth. It was a joy to fly, had no vices at all and could be thrown about in aerobatics as much as possible with plenty of power to get one out of a tight spot.

Peterborough was a good spot to be. It was easy to nip down to London by train for the weekend. Locally, the highlight was a Saturday evening dance at the local hotel with a live band. The mess was spacious and comfortable too.

So, after passing the test in Harts at Peterborough, we went on to the advanced training squadron at No 1 Flying Training School at one of the oldest of the RAF's aerodromes at Netheravon in Wiltshire. There we converted on to Hawker Hinds. These planes were very similar to the Harts except that while the Hart was basically a strike aircraft, the Hind was a bomber. However there was little difference in their appearance. They were just as friendly to fly.

And now the emphasis changed again. We had very little dual

(Left) The Author – Peterborough 1940. *(Right)* The Author and the Albacore at Arbroath.

David Foster, David Myles, Lyn Polwin and the Author at Sibsen, Peterborough.

flying with an instructor. Night flying, formation flying, cross-country flying, dive bombing and air to air attacks. It was an interesting and varied course where we were left much to our own initiative. One exercise for instance was to fly over to an airfield at Wroughton, carry out a reconnaissance and return with as much information as possible.

But we had our first fatal accidents at Netheravon. In the first, one of the course was taking off when another pupil landed on top of him. It was appallingly sad and shook all of us who were experiencing for the first time the loss of a friend. It was due to the non-observance of a golden rule – the plane taking off should stop at 90° to the direction of take-off and look both ways. Netheravon was, however, a very undulating grass airfield with no particular line of take-off and landing and he took a chance. The pilot who was landing was blind owing to the long engine housing in front of him.

The second loss was due to a new experience for us. The Battle of Britain was at its height while we were at Netheravon and Heinkel 111s, Junkers 88s and Messerschmitt 110s were not unusual in the skies thereabouts. One day in early October my Flight Commander told me that he wanted to go to Cranwell for lunch and stay overnight. Who better than me to fly the plane back to Netheravon. Good experience for you, he said by way of justification for him to attend a piss-up at Cranwell. The flight north was without incident. After a bite to eat, feeling like the golfer who turns up in the dining rooom at Sunningdale Golf Club in oily trousers, an open neck and no jacket, I took off to return to Netheravon. It was another lovely day. I decided to fly at 13,000 feet to enjoy the view.

Just over an hour later I landed at Netheravon and reported to Tower, only to find much panic there mixed with relief at getting one of their pilots back safely. There had apparently been a series of raids over Southern England and masses of Junkers and Messerschmitts had been too close to me for comfort and had been criss-crossing my line of flight. The Tower may have been worried but ignorance is bliss and I had enjoyed my day flying at 13,000 feet in a cloudless sky across England. However, another pilot on the course had not been so lucky and had been caught by a Messerschmitt while on a navigational exercise with no chance of survival.

The course rounded off with a fortnight's visit to Newton Down near Porthcawl in South Wales for an intensive training in air attack – or dog fights – and low and high dive bombing at targets off the coast.

The highlight, however, was the award of the Flying Badge – or wings – at the end of the course by the Group Captain commanding Netheravon. A proud moment indeed.

So that was the end of flying training as such and the RAF handed us over, so to speak, to the Navy. It was at this point that the course split between those wanting to be fighter pilots and those opting for the TBR or Torpedo Bomber Reconnaissance, part of the Fleet Air Arm. I don't quite know why, but I chose to be a TBR Pilot. Maybe I had a hunch that fighters were not for me or that I wasn't made for fighters. Anyway, there it was and I was due to go with some fifteen to twenty of the course to Scotland to join Naval training squadrons to be trained in the special disciplines of Naval flying. So, away with the bell-bottom trousers and the flat hat of a Naval rating and on with the reefer jacket, black tie and peak cap of a temporary Sub-Lieutenant (A) RNVR.

Instead, however, of carrying on with our training as fast as possible, bearing in mind the need for trained pilots in a situation where the country was fighting for its very life, we were sent off in common with all other newly commissioned officers to Royal Naval College Greenwich for a two week course to learn to be officers and gentlemen, otherwise known as the knife and fork course. Fine, I imagine in peacetime when there is plenty of time in which to indulge in such exercises but hardly suitable in a situation in which Europe had been overrun, France had capitulated, the disaster of Dunkirk had happened, the Battle of Britain had been fought and won and the country was about to be subjected to intense night bombing.

Such was this course that I have no memory of it except two aspects. Owing to the nightly bombing of London, we had to carry our bedding down to the cellars underneath the college where we slept every night. And the food; those were the days of shortages and rationing but the college food was some of the best I have ever seen anywhere before or since. All meals were taken in the Painted Hall and when it was a cold meal, it was a help yourself from tables that

ran along two of the walls at the top of the hall, carrying every type
of cold food that your mind can think up, all superbly served. Hot
meals were served by white-gloved, white tie stewards. I remember
going home on leave for the middle weekend of the course and feeling
the most intense embarrassment when I compared what my mother
had on which to feed the family and what I was consuming at
Greenwich. Still, maybe it made better pilots out of us.

And so to Naval flying training, first stop Crail Naval Air Station
which was situated on the bleak and cold east coast in Fife, Scotland,
near the headland of Fife Ness. We joined 786 Squadron which
conducted the Torpedo Training Course. The course lasted for two
of the coldest months that I can remember. East winds and blizzards
were normal. Snow was on the ground most of the time. Eighteen
hours' flying during that period was the result. As the name of the
course implies, almost all the eighteen hours in the air were spent
in all sorts of torpedo exercises, from camera attacks on a ship, each
flight lasting ten to twenty minutes, to a full scale torpedo attack in
formation from about 10,000 feet. The method of a torpedo attack
which was standard in the Navy, weather and cloud cover
permitting, was for the squadron or flight to approach at about
10,000 feet in a parallel line with the ship to be attacked. Vics of three
formations were usually adopted, their 'inside' plane moving across
to the other side of the leader just before the dive. The art that had
to be exercised by the leader was to start the dive at a point that
would end 50 feet above the sea immediately abeam of the ship. Each
of the three (followed by the next three and so on) would then turn
in fan-wise to the ship leaving them with as little run in as possible
before dropping the torpedoes or 'fish', this period and the get away
time being the period when the pilot was most vulnerable to fire from
the ship and attack by fighters. The pilot had to judge the speed of
the ship and 'lay off' the aircraft according to a pre-set torpedo aimer
consisting of a row of small bulbs across his line of vision on top of
the instruments' panel. The pilot also had to judge the size of the
ship so as to drop the torpedo in the right spot – not too close or too
far away.

I have heard this conversation shouted in times of panic down the
voice pipe at 10,000 feet:

Pilot to observer: 'Hey, Bill, is this the ship we're supposed to be attacking?'

Observer to pilot: 'Well, it is in the right place. Can't identify her though.'

Pilot to observer: 'OK let's go.' He jams the stick forward for the dive.

Observer to pilot: 'She's turning away to starboard.'

Pilot thinks: 'Bloody man – what do I do now. Think I'll attack from starboard side.'

Silence from the observer as he too is thinking.

Pilot swings the plane to starboard but the ship keeps turning.

Half way down in the screaming dive –

Pilot to observer: 'What's its speed?'

Observer to pilot: '25 knots, I should think. Camera switched on?'

Pilot to observer: 'Yes of course,' testily, but the ship is eluding him.

Pilot to observer: 'This is impossible, the bugger isn't co-operating.'

Pilot to observer: 'I'm bloody well overshooting. Can't see it now – it's under the wing somewhere – Oh Christ, what a balls up.' But just then the ship straightens.

Pilot to observer: 'Decent fellow. Am levelling off and turning in. God, we'll hit the sea soon. Height right – OK for lay off. Dropping now. Turn away aft.'

Pilot to observer: 'Give the skipper a wave – hope the camera worked.'

It sounds none too difficult in theory but, inevitably soon after committing oneself to the dive, the ship starts to alter course frantically and if you don't alter your approach, you may find yourself flying up its stern or down its funnel. And of course in the real thing, all the ship's guns would be blazing away at you – but you were supposed to ignore that factor. Finally the ship to be attacked would not be on its own but assuming it to be a battleship would be surrounded by cruisers and destroyers. To drop a torpedo effectively would entail flying over the outer and inner screen at the minimum height in a hail of ack-ack. I think I preferred the practice runs with a camera. In fact, in spite of all the training flights that I made during the war, I never did drop a torpedo in anger.

The planes we flew in the course were the Shark, Swordfish and

Albacore; a real come-down from the Hart and Hind. These were three of a long line of antiquated and ungainly naval aircraft that FAA pilots were expected to fly. They were out of date by 1939 and yet the Albacore made its debut in 1940 as a replacement for the Swordfish. In many cases of naval aircraft, the design of the manufacturers was reasonable but the boffins at the Admiralty then almost redesigned them to fit in with their apparent needs, with disastrous results. Equipment was added to the exterior of the plane as well as internally until the planes looked like a cross between a Christmas tree and a bathtub and ended up heavy and slow and in some cases positively dangerous. I can dismiss the Shark by saying that, thank God, I was only asked to fly it for one hour. I felt I was lucky to step out of it in one piece.

The Swordfish was a different matter. Although it was an out of date biplane soon after it saw the light of day in 1935 and painfully slow at a cruising speed of about 90 knots, it was perhaps aerodynamically the most perfect operational aeroplane of World War II. Was it the only plane in the world to be operational in 1939 and all the way through to 1945? I tried to make it spin from a stall but all I could get was a slow but upright and stable drop in height. It had no vices whatsoever. A lovely plane to fly with its short take-off and landing, immense manoeuvrability, wonderful reliability, and tough as old boots. The Stringbag was everyone's favourite. Its record in the war needs no elaborating.

I must not say too much against the Albacore as I was to fly it day and night for the next eighteen months and it was to save my life on a number of occasions. But although it was to replace the Swordfish, it was really an appalling failure. Its speed was only about 5 knots better than the Swordfish, whose manoeuvrability and reliability it certainly did not have. And if possible, it was uglier and more ungainly than the Swordfish. However, it did have one improvement; the crew were enclosed in a glasshouse, the pilot being perched up forward of the top plane and just behind the radial engine giving him a superb view. And it could carry one torpedo or mine, six 250 lb or four 500 lb bombs. It had two other advantages which were to appear later in operations. The engine was amazingly quiet when the prop was in coarse pitch, an asset when it came to night dive-bombing. And its speed was so slow that enemy ack-ack

David Foster and Edgar Russell at Arbroath.

'Coco' Brown, Eddie Carter and John Wilson at Arbroath.

gunners never did understand how such a plane could still be flying operational in 1941/42 and invariably put up their barrage well ahead of the aircraft. Its opportunity to achieve fame came during 1941 to 1943 in the Western Desert as a night dive bomber and as the first of the Pathfinders in a highly successful partnership with the Wellington.

From RNAS Crail we went further up the coast to RNAS Arbroath to join 767 Squadron to work up on other naval techniques and in particular deck landings. We were supposed to end the course by doing some landings on a carrier in the Clyde but this did not materialise and the course of a month's duration was confined to simulated deck landings on the runway – called ADDLS or Assisted Dummy Deck Landings.

One day, I was doing some exercise inland when I spied Glamis Castle below. The temptation was too great especially with its long drive up to the castle. So down I went, hopped over the gates, flew low up the drive and then pulled back hard to climb over and thankfully cleared the battlements. I was very satisfied as I flew back to Arbroath. Fortunately, Her Majesty The Queen was not in residence but the plane was of course spotted and reported. Two days later, a notice was circulated to all squadrons to the effect that aircraft will not, repeat not, fly in the vicinity of Glamis Castle. Disciplinary action will be taken against any pilot disobeying this order.

I remember flying a Gladiator here. This was the fastest plane I had so far flown – maximum speed of over 200 mph and very manoeuvrable. A real joy to fly.

I see, too, an entry in my logbook, 'Heathrow – Peterborough 1 hour 15 minutes', and the next day, 'Peterborough – Caterick – Arbroath'. I was collecting a new Albacore from Faireys Aviation, taking off from their small grass airfield now part of the airport. Against the official entry of the flight is a note that I made at the time 'New plane from Faireys – entertained well before taking off. Lovely weather and perfect visibility for Caterick to Arbroath.' No fear of being breathalized then and obviously the hangover had dispersed by the time I reached Caterick. This was lucky as I had called in at Peterborough for old times' sake and a few beers.

So, one year and 225 flying hours (154 solo) after joining the Navy at HMS St Vincent, my training as a Fleet Air Arm pilot had finished. Looking back, the training seems to have taken a long time, particularly bearing in mind the state of the war, the increasing danger that this country was facing and the pressing need for aircrew. However, clearly weather conditions, enemy air activity over Britain and the shortage of instructors played their part. Because of these factors, the whole of pilot training was soon to be transferred to Canada and the United States. But I was glad to have been able to do my training in this country. Where next then? Well, 'Go on leave and you will be told where to report to shortly.' So far, so good.

CHAPTER FOUR

The Cruise

It was not long before I was told that I was being posted to HMS Grebe, the aerodrome just outside Alexandria in Egypt that was the headquarters of the Fleet Air Arm in the Middle East. It was conveniently close to the harbour of Alexandria which was the base of the Eastern Mediterranean Fleet commanded by Admiral A.B. Cunningham.

This meant a dash to Messrs Gieves in Bond Street to get kitted out with tropical rig. So keen was I that I bought myself a white naval topee complete with tin box, as advised by Messrs Gieves as a protection from the tropical sun. The box was never opened until the end of the war when I threw it away! The standard headdress in Egypt was the ordinary naval cap with khaki and white covers as occasion demanded.

I was then told to report to SS *Georgic* in Greenock by the middle of May. Accordingly, with big tin box, suitcases, topee tin box and hand luggage, I made my way to Glasgow and reported to the OC Troops aboard *Georgic*.

Thus started one of the most extraordinary and bizarre journeys I have ever been on.

It did not take long after arrival on board to realise that *Georgic*, with *Britannic*, was one of the poshest liners of the White Star Fleet. She had not been converted to a troopship and was still in her immaculate condition as a passenger liner. I was allotted a twin berth cabin on one of the upper decks with all its sheets, fittings and trimmings, as for a peacetime voyage. The bars were all stocked with every kind of drink imaginable, complete with cocktail-shaking stewards, very smart in their white jackets. The dining room was laid out as if a peaceful voyage to New York was in prospect, again with a whole army of white-coated stewards.

I asked one of the bar stewards how the bars were so well stocked.

'Ah', he said, 'we have just come from Halifax, Nova Scotia, and made sure we stocked up fully. You never know when you will be able to stock up again.' As far as I know, no type of drink ran out during the five to six week voyage.

Finally, the meals had to be seen to be believed. The breakfast menu had every type of breakfast food one could think of. I remember the assortment of marmalades, jams and honey. Lunch and dinner were sumptuous and different every day. And this was 1941, when all the cities of England were being bombed relentlessly; we would be lucky to find a full blown meal with all the trimmings in the country in a private house or public restaurant. But if it is presented to you on a plate, why not sit down and enjoy it?

The Germans were at the Channel ports, they had taken Greece and were at that time invading Crete. Rommel had taken back the desert captured by Wavell and was a dangerous threat to the Middle East. But boy, was that steak good and here come the raspberries and cream.

As the ship filled up with passengers the variety of our fellow travellers became apparent. Top brass of all armed services were there as well as the small fry such as the twelve or so who represented the Fleet Air Arm. An Admiral led the rankings. There were Queen Alexandria nurses, Wrens, Waaf and ATS Officers. All the officers of a County Regiment, the troops of which filled the holds in appalling conditions. There were also a number of civilians, including some showbiz personalities, who were going out to the Middle East to join ENSA, the organisation for entertaining the troops.

But for the next ten days, that is where the glamour stopped. We sailed from the Clyde on 21st May and joined up with our convoy which consisted of nine large troopships and merchantmen. A lovely prize for any U-boat. Imagine our dismay when our escort joined us consisting of four of Vian's famous destroyers, *Cossack*, *Maori*, *Sikh* and *Zulu*, another destroyer together with two cruisers, the *Cairo* and the *Exeter* (of Battle of the River Plate fame). Nevertheless, small protection for such a convoy. Unknown to us, the aircraft carrier *Victorious* and the battle-cruiser *Repulse* should also have been escorting us. The reason for their absence was that a few hours after our departure, and unknown to us, *Bismarck* and the *Prinz Eugen* left the Norwegian coast for their dash via the Denmark Straits into the Atlantic.

All this is now well known, but at the time, we were only aware of our comfort inboard, the appalling weather of rain, mist and rough seas outboard and a certain apprehension that we were going into the unknown, the inhospitable Atlantic and the U-boats waiting poised to catch a prey like us.

All seemed to go reasonably well until the 24th by which time, the convoy had turned on to a southerly course and was off the west of Ireland. We were then told over the tannoy that the *Bismarck* was steaming through the Denmark Straits between Iceland and Greenland and soon afterwards that HMS *Hood* had been sunk. This put everyone in a large state of depression but life onboard and particularly the eating and drinking continued as usual. None was really aware of the possible dangers to the convoy from that direction – and the Denmark Straits seemed a long way away.

However, by the afternoon of 25th May, a bombshell hit the passengers. The tannoy announced that *Bismarck* would pass 30 miles astern of the convoy during the coming night. It didn't need much of an imagination to foresee the ghastly danger we were in. We did not know that she was being chased and encircled by the Navy and that she was making almost certainly for Brest. We did know that she had been sent into the Atlantic to sink convoys like ours. What was 30 miles in the Atlantic with the convoy doing a steady 13 knots and *Bismarck* capable of 30 and all of 42,000 tons of her and eight 15" guns. I don't think I have ever seen such instantaneous or mob-like panic as that which immediately hit all of us passengers. There was a mad and barbaric dash for the bars. Sheer fear of a cornered animal gripped everyone. Stiff drinks were ordered and drunk like water to be repeated and repeated till depression and morbid fear set in. Every man (and woman) for himself.

Rumours started and grew with the telling, 'One of the ship's officers has just told me ...' Speculation was rife. Some would have us in the sea already swimming for our lives. Some would reminisce about the effect of 15" shells. We were doomed already, drowned in the rough, dark and oily Atlantic. There was not much sleep that night aboard SS *Georgic*, unless it was in a drunken stupor. One could only feel sorry for the ship's crew and particularly the agony that must have gripped those on the bridge. No alcoholic escape for them. They had no alternative but to keep station and plug away at 13 knots in the hope that death and destruction would not suddenly rush and roar towards the convoy in the shape of 15" shells from *Bismarck*.

Worse was to come. Next morning, not a single destroyer was to be seen – there was only the convoy and the diminutive *Exeter*. Rumours and hangovers were rife; the sea looked uninviting and the future non-existent.

We were soon put out of our misery. The tannoy told us that destroyers had been called away to help with the tracking and destruction of *Bismarck*. Later, the Fleet Air Arm Swordfish from *Ark Royal* had hit and slowed *Bismarck*. Our little party of FAA pilots and observers felt 12 feet tall at that moment. Then on 27th May we were told that *Bismarck* had been sunk. Again, a stampede to the bars. Just as much, if not more, was drunk this time but in jubilation and relief. I couldn't help noticing the difference between these incidents and one that I had experienced in London during the night bombing of the City. Then, as the sirens blared away, I had to walk from Waterloo to King's Cross to catch a train to Scotland, as the tube wasn't running. I had had to throw myself into a muddy gutter on the north side of Waterloo Bridge when the increasingly noisy whine announced the imminent arrival of a stack of bombs. Soon, the whole of the West End seemed to be ablaze and the noise of fire and crumbling buildings accompanied the screaming of fire engines and ambulances. I was glad to get under the roof of a pub in Shaftesbury Avenue. It was packed. The noise was deafening both inside and out. There was not, however, the blind panic and free for all stampede of *Georgic* but the laughter, jokes and friendship, and 'the bombs are not going to upset our sense of humour' attitude. Perhaps being surrounded by sea and its watery grave made all the difference to our feelings and behaviour on *Georgic*.

The *Bismarck* may have been sunk but we were in the thick of the U-boat area. Nobody was smiling yet. In due time we made Freetown for refuelling and the knowledge that the rest of the voyage should be relatively trouble-free. We were soon in the tropics. Another indication of the luxury of the cruiser became apparent. *The dansant* began on the Promenade Deck to a six piece band and continued every afternoon for the rest of the voyage. On Saturday evenings formal full dress dances were held in the saloon. And the parties, the drinking and the eating continued unabated. *Georgic*'s larder and wine cellars seemed inexhaustible. Was there really a war on? The *Bismarck* incident was soon forgotten too. Midsummer weekend was spent in Durban. Then the run up the East Coast of Africa through the Red Sea with a following wind like a sauna bath, and at last we arrived at Suez.

We were packed and ready to disembark on to what looked like an inhospitable shore. Goodbyes were being said all round. I remember so vividly, one of the short snatches of conversation. I was leaning over the rails on the upper deck, musing at this country, the like of which I had not seen before. The dust, the filth, the shambles, lack of order, everything happening at a snail's pace with apparently no aim in view, when along came a member of the crew whom I recognised as the librarian, taking the air, still smart in his white jacket and dark trousers.

'How did you think the voyage went?' I asked him. 'I expect you're glad to have a bit of a rest.'

'Yes indeed. We were lucky weren't we, but it seemed to go well. You know, I have been a member of the crew since *Georgic* first put to sea. I must say that I have never been on a voyage where there has been so much boozing and after all this boat was built for boozing.'

I thought this was one way of describing the last few weeks. Five days later the *Georgic* was bombed and badly damaged by fire in an Italian air raid on Suez. The Italian airmen had succeeded where the *Bismarck* and U-boats had failed. Was this retribution by the gods?

CHAPTER FIVE

The Desert

So I joined 826 Squadron at Dekheila at the end of July 1941 feeling very much the junior in a squadron of highly experienced air-crew. It was a new world of operational flying after training. There was a feeling of doing something positive at last. I was back on Albacores, given aircraft R for Roger and assigned to Y Flight. The squadron acquired a new CO, Lieutenant Commander 'Jack' Corbett RN, and its senior observer was Lieutenant 'Pinkie' Haworth RN. Both seemed at the time to be old enough to be a different generation though there was only a few years between us. Jack Corbett was god as far as I was concerned. All the other pilots and observers were within a year or two of my age. About half were RN(A) or 'A' Boys – holders of short service commissions in the Air Branch of the Navy and the rest were RNVR. My observer was Sub-Lieutenant McIntosh, a South African, and my airgunner was Leading Airman Harper. Mac and I were to stay together for the next twelve months; Harper left the squadron in April 1942 when long range petrol tanks were fitted in the observer's cockpit. My Flight Commander was Sub-Lieutenant (A) 'Ferret' Ellis RN; 'Ferret' because he looked like one. He was thin, with ginger hair and a pointed thin face, a man of few words, never a smile to relieve his serious countenance. He was, however, completely dedicated to flying which he practised with correctness. With a single-minded keenness he taught me a lot and I counted myself lucky to have him as my Flight Commander. I was very sad when I heard that he had been killed while flying off a carrier later in the war.

The squadron ground crews were mostly naval ratings, who made up the fitters, riggers, armourers, etc., but the head of each 'trade' was an RAF sergeant. And in charge of the ground crews was Flight Sergeant Stinchcombe. He ruled the squadron or rather, the

maintenance side, with an organising ability and professionalism
which inspired his ratings and resulted in the most efficient possible
maintenance of the aircraft. He never shouted, never lost his cool,
was always firm but fair. The squadron was lucky to have him in
charge on the ground. His relationship with us young pilots was that
of headmaster and young irresponsible and ignorant pupils. There
was an obvious and natural feeling of superiority in him tempered
only slightly with a touch of deference. To report an ailing machine
to Flight Sergeant Stinchcombe was like going to the dentist. The
aircraft would have all sorts of things wrong with it until one came
face to face with 'Sir'. Then one wondered why one was there at all.
The defects were hard to explain in the face of his cross-questioning.
You got the impression that you were criticising his own handiwork.
The pilot invariably ended up apologising for being a nuisance.
However, he always produced an amazingly high degree of
serviceability in spite of the ravages of sand. And sand was to be our
constant headache in the desert. The planes were always parked in
the open with no protection from the eternal sand. Engine covers
didn't seem to help as the sand got into every nook and cranny. It
is a wonder that we were able to achieve the serviceability that we
did, thanks largely to the loving care given by the ground crews.

It wasn't long before we knew our fate. It was for the squadron
to go up to the desert to make its base at an airfield called Ma'aten
Bagush Satellite. This desolate spot was about 120 miles west of
Dekheila and some 30 miles east of Mersa Matruh. Ma'aten Bagush
main airfield was alongside the one and only road which followed
the coast from Alexandria to Benghazi via Mersa Matruh and
Tobruk. The satellite airfield was a mile or so inland from the road
and positioned on top of the low escarpment that ran parallel with
the road as far as the boundary with Cyrenaica. The airfield only
consisted of a roughly levelled square piece of sand but it boasted
two ramshackle wooden huts, one was to be the officers' mess and
the other was for the ground crews. Levelling only meant that the
camel scrub, which were low round pieces of vegetation about a foot
high and two feet across, was removed. Otherwise the airfield was
just a fairly flat piece of sand. It was not the type of sand found on
a beach but more like grit and quite stony.

The squadron took all its planes to the desert together with a

The Author and 'R' for Robert at Dekheila – August 1941.

(Left) David Foster at Dekheila. *(Right)* My observer, Denis McIntosh at Dekheila.

View towards Alex from mess at Dekheila.

Tug Wilson and Bobby Bradshaw on mess terrace – Dekheila.

skeleton maintenance team. Small repairs could be undertaken in the desert but anything of a major nature entailed a flight back to Dekheila where the main maintenance crews stayed under the eagle eye of Flight Sergeant Stinchcombe. In any case, a plane and its aircrew would return to Dekheila about every five weeks for servicing for the plane and a bath – a spot of comfort for the aircrew. Groundcrews were swapped round regularly.

Life was pretty basic in the desert. All personnel slept in tents dispersed round the huts. Pilot and observer shared a tent in case of an emergency call at night. Although the huts were ramshackle and wooden, we soon made them as comfortable as we could with a bar made out of flare and bomb boxes and a mess separated from the bar by curtains. The food was salt beef in all its forms augmented by supplies from base. And the crew of every flight from Dekheila was under orders to load every corner of the plane with goodies and especially booze. One thing was certain – the bar was never to run dry and nor did it.

The tents were basic too and were equipped with the most uncomfortable camp beds imaginable. We collected and put together furniture of flare and bomb boxes, as required. On the other hand, our clothing was minimal. Khaki shorts, shirts, socks and desert boots. A change to khaki trousers for flying as a protection against fire and a sweater or two since the night air at 10,000 feet could be distinctly chilly. Even on the ground in winter, the nights could be quite cold, sometimes very wet and on one occasion we even had a day of sleet. As time went on dress became less naval (though at the beginning it was only just regulation) and more civilian. Coloured sweaters and multi-coloured scarves were the fashion. Two 'musts' however were the rank on the shoulder strap and the ever worn naval cap with khaki cover. Otherwise an onlooker could be forgiven for assuming that the aircrew were a bunch of mercenaries rather than a crack Naval Air Squadron.

There were, however, one or two pluses in the desert. Strangely enough it was a healthy place in spite of the ever-present flies. Sandfly fever was about the only disease that regularly plagued us. Apart from flies, there were no livestock – or almost none. I do remember one night when we were attacked by German bombers. Mac and I jumped out of our beds on hearing the tell-tale sound of the engines. We were about to dive into the slit trench that every tent had beside it when we saw in the moonlight a black scorpion at the bottom of it. We chose to face the bombs rather than this deadly little creature and got back to bed. The bombs only displaced some sand, the scorpion remained undisturbed and we got our sleep.

The other live animal was rather more unexpected. Mac and I had been away up the desert at Sidi Barrani and beyond on the usual operations for a couple of days. On our return, after we had had breakfast, we wandered over to the tent to crash out in our beds. As we pulled aside the flap there was a distinct movement behind the beds and the flare box furniture in between. A fat scaley back appeared; then its long tail and finally its head. Mac, who was obviously used to such revelations in South Africa whipped out his revolver and shot the animal in the head. It shook this off and went on moving. A second shot finished it off. We dragged it out and displayed our prize outside the mess – a four foot long iguana. Goodness only knows where it had come from; it was the only one we saw. Mac took it all as part of the day's work but I had no sleep that day.

There was no bull or traditional naval discipline; that is not to say there was a lack of discipline, but the atmosphere could be said to be relaxed. And when anything to do with flying was concerned, discipline was present in no uncertain terms; it was self-imposed, or shall we say, it came down from god, sitting in the CO's office (a tent on the far side of the airfield).

The military position in the desert in July 1941 was fairly static. Wavell had led his magnificent advance at the end of 1940 and beginning of the following year, first of all against the Italians entrenched at Sidi Barrani. This developed into a full scale rout as far as El Agheila, south of Benghazi. But Greece was erupting and men and machines were sent there, thus depleting the desert force with a long line of communication to deal with as well. A perfect situation for Rommel and his Panzer divisions and he used it to the full. The British forces were pushed back to the Egyptian frontier, or 'the wire' as it was known, leaving only Tobruk holding out deep inside enemy territory. A fruitless attempt had been made in June 1941 to relieve Tobruk. Rommel had counter-attacked and entered Egypt for a short distance but withdrew leaving the situation as it

(Left) Jeff Powell and the Author at Ma'aten Bagush Satellite. *(Right)* Lucky Sutton at Dekheila.

The Author, 'Body' Corpes and Tattersall at Ma'aten Bagush Satellite.

was before. It transpired, after we had moved to Ma'aten Bagush, that General Auchinleck, who had taken Wavell's place, was planning a fullscale attack later in the year.

So, when the squadron finally moved with petrol bowsers, lorries, stores and basic ground crew to Ma'aten Bagush satellite at the end of August, the dividing line between British and German forces was the wire with Halfaya Pass and Sollum in German hands and Buq Buq and Sidi Barrani in British territory. Sidi Barrani was to be our forward airfield for refuelling on the way out and again on the way back when the flying time inside enemy territory made it necessary. It was about 120 miles west of Ma'aten Bagush so that the squadron's desert base was about halfway between Alexandria and the wire.

The squadron's role was a strange one. At first only the barest outline was laid down. It was left to develop as occasion demanded and performance and circumstances permitted. The Navy were loath to second the squadron completely to the RAF. So, it was agreed that naval command in Alex would have first priority in the use of the squadron in cases where the Navy would regard the particular operation to be theirs, as for instance, spotting for naval bombardment, bomb or torpedo attacks on the Italian fleet, if it ever got within range, or anti-submarine patrols. If the Navy did not want us, we were at the disposal of the RAF for night dive bombing on German and Italian airfields. The Army began to take an interest in us. They were impressed by our ability to navigate over the desert. Fleet Air Arm observers were trained to navigate over the sea. The same skills applied to the desert which had no landmarks. We therefore began to get work from the Army in reconnoitering behind enemy lines at night to look for concentrations of armour, transport, camps, etc. At first we operated with the help of the moon but later we developed our own techniques with flares. We usually carried incendiary and high explosive bombs as well so that we could have a go if we found anything. On most nights there were up to half a dozen Albacores from 826 Squadron flying around the night sky between Bardia and Gazala, dropping flares and looking for any likely evidence of Army activity and bombing possible targets such as airfields. If we did nothing else, many of the enemy would have had sleepless nights.

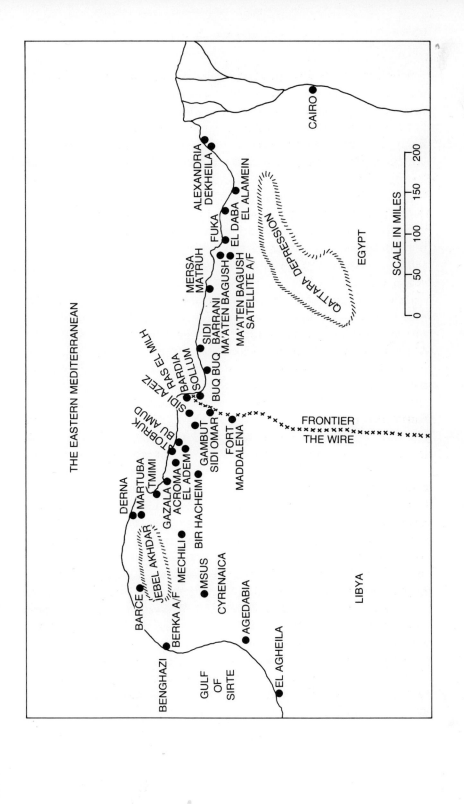

THE EASTERN MEDITERRANEAN

BENGHAZI
BARCE
DERNA
MARTUBA
TMIMI
BERKA A/F
JEBEL AKHDAR
GAZALA
ACROMA
MECHILI
EL ADEM
BIR HACHEIM
MSUS
GAMBUT
SIDI OMAR
CYRENAICA
FORT
MADDALENA
AGEDABIA
GULF
OF
SIRTE
EL AGHEILA
LIBYA

TOBRUK
BU AMUD
SIDI AZEIZ
RAS EL MDAUUAR
BARDIA
SOLLUM
BUQ BUQ
SIDI
BARRANI
MA'ATEN BAGUSH
SATELLITE A/F

MERSA
MATRUH
FUKA
EL DABA
ALEXANDRIA
DEKHEILA
EL ALAMEIN

QATTARA DEPRESSION

EGYPT

CAIRO

FRONTIER
THE WIRE

SCALE IN MILES
0   50   100   150   200

And so, as the work and targets developed, the squadron would develop its techniques, methods and sometimes its hardware. We were on our own far from home with no control from above as to how we achieved our objectives. An example of a change in the hardware resulted from an early realisation that an H-E bomb merely dug itself into the sand and removed a ton or two to another part of the desert. We therefore hit upon the idea of screwing an iron rod about three feet long into the nose of the bomb. The other end of the rod would have a flat, round base. The bomb would therefore explode some foot or two above ground spraying shrapnel in all directions. Very useful when bombing parked aircraft, tanks and transport.

Perhaps the most significant development of techniques was in the use of flares. At first a plane would bomb on its own flares. This however meant that the pilot had little time between dropping the flare and starting his bombing dive. The method was changed so that two or more planes operated together, one or two providing the flares, while the others bombed through them. We then moved to a situation where we provided the flare dropping for Wellingtons to bomb through the flares. This resulted from the RAF recognising the superiority of the Naval observers in navigating to targets in the desert. Flying over the desert was very similar to flying over the sea. The RAF bombers were not equipped for navigating over either sea or desert nor were their navigators trained for it. On the other hand the Naval observer was trained to navigate over the sea and this training came in very useful in the desert. So, it was the obvious step for us to find the target, lead the heavy bombers to it and then provide the illumination.

This method did have some cause for apprehension for us. We would drop the flares from about 8,000 feet; the Wellingtons flew much higher so that they would be bombing the targets not only through the flares but through us. We were therefore vulnerable from above as well as below. A veritable fly-berger. But we couldn't get the hell out of it when the Wellingtons came along as the flares needed constant topping-up to provide continuous illumination. The Wellingtons were based in the Delta area so that all briefing of the two squadrons, and timing, had to be done on the old fashioned and crackly telephone. Nevertheless, the operations were highly successful and the Wellingtons were delighted to be guided to the target by our flares and on arrival to have the desert looking like daylight. Were we the original Pathfinders? Certainly 826 Squadron and the Wellingtons hit on the same idea in the desert in 1941 as was used to such good effect over Germany by Bomber Command and the famous Pathfinders later in the war.

The Albacore for all its faults, certainly had its year or so of glory in 1941 to 1943 in the Western Desert. True it couldn't be used in daylight owing to its speed. It was however especially good for looking for dive-bombing targets in the desert at night.

Its slowness was an asset in locating targets; it was quiet, especially in the dive with the prop at coarse pitch, and manoeuvrable too. It was a rugged plane that could take a lot of punishment and robust enough for landing on unlikely desert airfields. The speed of the Albacore – 90-95 knots – fully laden had unexpected results. In approaching a well defended target, such as an airfield at 10,000 feet, the heavy ack-ack would open up. But the gunners obviously thought they had a faster plane to contend with as the ack-ack was always well ahead of the plane they were shooting at. The same thing happened when we came within range of the light ack-ack.

Judging by the abuse that was handed out by the German and Italian forces and even Rome Radio, we were successful. In the early days, Rommel thought our secret weapon was a new form of helicopter. Some helicopter. The Germans however never quite got the hang of this phenomenon that flew around the sky over the desert on most nights; sometimes singly, sometimes in pairs and often in concerted full scale attacks. The plane was quiet and slow and therefore in the dark, somewhat eerie. Flares would light up the desert seemingly from nowhere. Later, this as often as not meant a full and concentrated bombing raid by Wellingtons. But in the early days it might or might not mean a stick of bombs across a camp or airfield.

The desert itself was an amazing area. It had a simplicity of landscape all of its own. It was in fact just miles and miles of sand as far as the eye could see. So it should have given the impression of ugliness or boredom. There were only four parallel features; the coast where the Southern Mediterranean lapped peacefully on to white sandy beaches; a road from Alexandria all the way through

Egypt, to the wire or boundary with Cyrenaica and onwards to
Tobruk, Benghazi and Tunisia; the railway from Alexandria to the
rail-head just east of the wire; and a low escarpment five miles in
from the coast which ran as far as the wire. Apart from the small
towns of Mersa Matruh, Bardia, Tobruk and Derna, there were no
habitations and apart from the camel scrub which looked dead
anyway, no vegetation. Nothing moved upon this sandy waste other
than the odd train and infrequent army lorries on the road. Stark,
forbidding, lonely and desolate would all be apt descriptions of this
piece of the earth's surface, apparently forsaken by God as if he had
run out of ideas. But perhaps he hadn't run out of ideas. Perhaps,
he designed this corner of his new world to show that beauty is not
necessarily spectacular and colourful. And yet the desert was all
these things with a strange beauty all of its own. When it was
analysed, it defied real description but it could not be ignored; it was
simple but at the same time complex. It haunts the memory of forty
years. It seems to hold a riddle, but what? It compels attention, but
why? And it commands respect, but how?

Usually the sun beat down relentlessly so that the wadis in small
river valleys were parched. But the desert could show its teeth when
something upset it. A sandstorm was the most unpleasant thing to
be experienced. Shelter was useless as the sand was driven into every
corner, not to mention the mouth and eyes. Rain could be a deluge
lasting a night and leaving the desert temporarily like a vast lake.
And it could be bitterly cold. I remember sleet falling steadily and
heavily one November day.

Its finest mood seemed to be at dawn. During the period from
August 1941, when we went up to the desert on a permanent footing,
throughout Christmas, we would often have to take off from Ma'aten
Bagush at about 4 pm to make Sidi Barrani before dark for
refuelling. Then after dark, off we would go for our nightly prowling
over Gambut, Bardia, Gazala or Derna returning to Sidi Barrani for
further petrol and a welcome cup of tea, even if it was made with
brackish water. At first light we would take off again for home base,
which meant beer and eggs and bacon before turning in for a good
zizz. I remember especially the flight back into the dawn from Sidi
Barrani. Soon after take-off the Eastern sky would seem to explode
into a mass of the most fantastic colours streaking above the desert.

The colours would be reflected on the desert itself which seemed to take on a fresh look as if covered with dew. The colours kept changing imperceptibly until the red rim of the sun appeared over the horizon. It was in those few minutes that the desert disclosed its strangest of strange beauties. On these occasions I would undo the straps, lean back, light a forbidden cigarette, feel contented with a night's work successfully completed and take in this miracle of colours.

CHAPTER SIX

To The Desert

So we moved up to the desert in August 1941. Convoys of lorries carried the minimum ground crews necessary for a forward base, fitters and riggers for each plane, armourers, a store keeper and very small office staff. The aircrews ferried up in several flights to Ma'aten Bagush Satellite such stores that could be carried by air. We all did several trips. Meanwhile, work went on to make Bagush as habitable as possible in the circumstances. We were lucky in having the two large wooden shacks which were soon basically furnished, tents put up in a dispersed fashion round the huts, latrines dug and dispersal points cleared round the perimeter of the airfield for the aircraft; as far away from each other for safety from a bomb attack. We were vulnerable to bombing from Heinkel 111 and Ju88s based in Crete and over the wire in Cyrenaica. We kept all of the squadron's twelve Albacores at Bagush other than those requiring repairs that could not be done in the desert and those requiring servicing, and a rest for the aircrew, in effect a decent bed and a chance to get the sand out of the hair. Depending on operational requirements, the number at Dekheila at any one time might have been between one and three and the duration of our stay between one and five days. If operations demanded it, a crew would take a plane to Dekheila in the morning and bring back a spare in the afternoon ready for the night's operations.

It soon became clear that life in the desert was coloured and influenced by three telling factors. The first was common to all three services and that was the lack of bull already mentioned. Discipline there certainly was but it was not the traditional sort as found in King's Regulations and Admiralty Instructions. We made our own discipline emanating from the fight to survive against the elements and against the enemy. It was not Naval discipline from the book, which could only have led to frustration, but an *esprit de corps*.

Everyone co-operated to make life as comfortable and cheerful against the odds and this was reflected in the quality of the operations.

The second factor also common to everyone in the desert was the feeling borne of the geography of the area of operations. We seemed to be fighting a private war in an area cut off from the centre of operations by the Mediterranean, uninfluenced by the world at large and confined to a strip of land some 10-12 miles in width and 300 miles in length. There were two very similar and equal opponents. The fighting was tough and relentless but somehow each side knew the other, respected the other and acted towards the other in some sort of gentlemanly way – a modern jousting match. Perhaps the wire running south from Sollum in a straight line along the border between Egypt and Cyrenaica albeit just a coil of barbed wire had psychologically something to do with it. Perhaps it was the result of the fact that there were no civilians to get killed or maimed and no private dwellings to be destroyed. The leaders of their respective armies could well have influenced the outlook of their forces – Wavell, Auchinleck and Rommel. There was a story that a British pilot was forced to land behind the lines. He destroyed his plane and set off to walk to the British lines, not knowing where he was except that his rough course could only be east. Alas, he was caught by the Germans and for some reason taken before Rommel personally. Rommel treated him with the utmost courtesy even congratulating him in his efforts to escape before he handed him over to his captors. In fact Rommel was held in such respect by the British troops that Auchinleck was forced to issue an Order of the Day reminding the troops that he was the enemy. Nonetheless, the British forces adopted the favourite German song of Lili Marlene.

Finally, there was the atmosphere in 826 Squadron itself. There can be little doubt that from top to bottom, it was one of the happiest squadrons of the war. In the paradoxically confined situation at desert airfields, there was no importance in rank from the CO down to the most junior fitter and yet everyone knew his place and his role. The pride of the ground crews in their particular plane and the concern they showed for all their planes and the aircrew's performance was outstanding. Belly-aching there was but it was always jovial and laughter wasn't far away.

And the aircrews, to a man, got on together; there wasn't a misfit or awkward cuss among them. This was amazing considering that when not on ops, there was only the uncomfortable wooden mess to meet in. No run ashore to the girlfriend from Bagush. No fleshpots nearby. It is fair to say that thanks to frequent trips by one plane or another to Dekheila, we never ran out of drink and cigarettes even though the former were not always of the best quality and the latter were inevitably foul. The food was grim too though at one point we were lucky enough to secure the services of the former Chief Chef of the Adlon Hotel, Berlin. What he could do with our staple diet, bully beef, would not have disgraced the Ritz. Every meal suddenly became a delight to look forward to.

But it was the people who made the atmosphere, the friendships which in many cases have lasted ever since even to a reunion well attended every year now entering its 39th year. Letters continue to come in from all over the globe and visits from Australia and New Zealand are frequent. The camaraderie, the cooperation, the laughter and the fun were something to be experienced. And above all, a pride in being a member of 826 was reflected on the ground and in the air alike.

The CO, Jack Corbett, and Senior Observer Pinkie Haworth blended their positions of authority with a readiness to live in with the rest of us. Discipline, or as much as was necessary, hardly had to be enforced, the quiet word was all that was necessary. Two other older members of the squadron were also like father figures to us younger ones. Flight Lieutenant Robbie Robertson from Adelaide was our Intelligence Officer but did much more in organising this and that around the place. Doc Duncan, a gynaecologist by speciality, found himself the doctor to an unlikely band of unruly aircrew in a strange operating theatre. I didn't think we stretched his medical knowledge or experience but he was invaluable as our father confessor, a sounding board for any moans and groans.

Then there was the primus inter paras – Bobbie Bradshaw. He joined the squadron at the time of its formation in 1940 as a midshipman, stayed with the squadron for three years ending up as its CO and a Lieutenant-Commander. He was without doubt one of the finest operational pilots thrown up by the FAA in World War II as well as being an outstanding personality with a very strong

(Right) Bobby Bradshaw.

(Below) Robby Robertson, Sid Revett, Denis McIntosh, the Author and Lucky Sutton at the mess at Dekheila – 1942.

individuality of his own. He became a legend far beyond the confines of the FAA. After 826 he did great things off carriers in the North Sea. He thus spent 4½ years almost continuously in operations being awarded the DSC and two bars and being mentioned three times in dispatches.

Behind this record, was an extraordinary person. A touch of the aristocrat and the born leader, combined with an individuality and a happy-go-lucky disposition, made Bradshaw a personality in any surroundings. He was always colourful, often crazy and generally a larger than life extrovert. But with all this he had a singular modesty of his own.

He had no regard whatever for authority rules or convention. Fortunately, like T.E. Lawrence, the desert was made for him ... No formal naval discipline, a casualness in dress and night operations that gave scope for individual initiative, all suited him down to the ground. He had one governing ambition – to cause as much damage to the enemy as possible. On at least two occasions when we were near enough to the German forces to do two operations each night, Bobby did three – without the consent of the CO of course.

Not far behind Bobby in flying ability and flair for the individual action was Lucky Sutton. He was a law unto himself and a dare devil pilot. Like Bobby, he could make the Albacore do anything. They were a flying circus duet.

The aircrew who had been out on ops the night before would catch up on sleep in the morning, carry out necessary squadron duties in the afternoon or join the bathing party bound for one of the lovely beaches nearby, then a change from shorts to khaki trousers against the evening chill and repair to the mess for beer and grub. This was followed by more beer and then a few music hall turns from Robbie Robertson our Australian Intelligence Officer with his rendering of 'The Death of Nelson' to Richard Hayes reciting his own poems. Lucky Sutton would chip in with a turn or two. Boredom didn't exist even in this outlandish place.

CHAPTER SEVEN

Desert Operations

During my stay in the squadron, its life was roughly divided into two parts. From August 1941 to the turn of the year we were involved in the preparations for General Auchinleck's attack *Crusader* to capture Cyrenaica and then if possible Tripolitania. The routine in the squadron was for the CO to phone Naval group headquarters in the morning to find out whether we would be required to attack a naval target along the coast. More often than not, the answer was negative. The CO then offered our service to the RAF and the Army who always had plenty on offer. Details would be given over the phone and the operation worked out by the CO and Pinkie Haworth during the morning. Sometimes, if it was an important target or a piece of vital reconnaissance, Army officers would come to Bagush to brief us personally and often would stay on until the return of the aircraft to get the information first hand.

My first op ended in disaster. It was an attack by most of the squadron on a submarine that was supposed to be alongside in Bardia Harbour. It seemed that we were always being asked to attack Bardia during the next five months. The name of the place became boring mainly because we never seemed to achieve anything. Bardia was a small frontier town on top of high cliffs, at the bottom of which was a tiny harbour behind a Cornish type jetty. The harbour could only take the smallest coastal boat or a submarine and the stores that could be landed there were minimal. One felt that the Naval authorities, looking for something for us to do for them, could come up with nothing better than 'Send them to Bardia tonight.'

My job in this first op was to be stand-by flamedropper to Bertie Blacow, an old hand and very experienced. Seeing my nervousness, he took great pains to 'nurse' me before take-off. 'Just follow me but if you lose me do your own thing and don't worry – they may throw some shit at the bombers but we should be all right at 10,000 feet. Bomb after me and if you are in any doubt about fuel after the attack, land at Sidi Barrani.'

We took off at dusk from Bagush, the bombers in their own formation, Bertie Blacow and I together and apart from the others. It was a pitch black night but the breaking wash along the coastline could be easily seen. We carried four 250 lb bombs and as many flares as we could carry. We climbed along the coast to Barrani and across the bay to Bardia to 10,000 feet. At the prearranged time Bertie dropped his first two flares to light up Bardia like daylight. The rest of the squadron were beginning to dive bomb the harbour. The searchlights came on and the ack-ack began. Multi coloured tracer lazily climbing into the night sky like Roman candles at a fairground. And we up there were seemingly suspended in air and on a piece of string – a kind of Aunt Sally. I had lost Bertie but having counted his flares, knew that he must have dived with his bombs.

I suddenly felt alone but at the same time horribly responsible for Mac my observer and Harper my airgunner in the back. At least there was someone to talk to. 'Starting to drop flares, Mac.' 'OK' came his reply. We did passes across Bardia until all our flares were exhausted. 'Going into bombing run, Mac.' 'OK.'

I positioned myself to the west of Bardia in order to make the getaway over the sea and opposite the friendly coast. Coarse pitch to keep the engine noise to a minimum, throttle back, bombs armed, and flap partially down to act as air brakes, wing over and nose down. Lined up with Bardia first above the engine cowling. A relief to feel the exhilaration of speed after stooging around in the dark at 90 knots. The flak and searchlights were in front of us and therefore no problem. 8,000 feet ... 6,000 feet ... 4,000 feet and at 3,000 feet started to lift the nose just above the target and released the bombs at 2-2,500 feet. Turned first left and then right to deceive the following tracer but kept going down to keep up speed. Straddled the town and harbour but could not see any submarine. However ... a sigh of relief that that was over and no damage to the aircraft.

'Mac, we'll have to land at Barrani – fuel low.' 'OK.' We found the airfield across the bay and there were four or five lamps in a line that called itself a flamepath. I had never been there before. The sand was an impossible surface at night on which to judge height.

Nor did the small lamps help. But there was really no excuse for coming in too fast and too low resulting in writing off the undercart and prop and skidding to a grinding halt. I felt like a bit of chewed up string when I climbed out and jumped down in the darkness. I had visions of being handed my papers with the note, 'He only did one operation and wrote off a plane in the process.' My humiliation was saved by Jeff Powell, another old timer who had landed at Barrani too. 'Not to worry, difficult landing conditions, bloody awful flarepath, could have happened to anyone.'

I felt better but knew that the day of reckoning was not far off when I had to report to the CO, Jack Corbett. After telling him what happened, he seemed to take an understanding and lenient view, asking me mainly about the attack. 'Still, we'd better have a night landing test.'

So, with the CO at the end of the runway at Dekheila, I did half a dozen night landings – successfully. When I parked the plane, the CO sauntered across saying, 'Well done, there is no problem in landing an Albacore at night, is there? Let's forget everything and get on with the job in hand.' I felt that day that I had really become a member of 826.

We were to do five more attacks on shipping at Bardia before the year was out. The second one a month later was memorable for two twists. I got to 10,000 feet and was suddenly overtaken by an attack of gyppy tummy. Well, I've had gyppy tummy in most situations but only once strapped into an Albacore, sitting on my parachute, an hour and a half from home at 10,000 feet. 'Please, sir, I want to be excused' sprang to mind but was soon discarded. 'Feeling bloody, Peter.' Peter Wellington was flying with me that night instead of Mac. 'Anything I can do?' says he. 'Will have to go to the gents soon,' said I. 'Well not here, old boy.' 'Maybe not, but I'm not sticking around any longer' and with that I dropped all the flares and almost before they lit up I started diving, as steeply and fast as possible. I dropped my two 500 and two 250 pounders and ran for Bagush full throttle at all of 105 knots. I missed the harbour but hit and set fire to a large building. The final straw was that Rome Radio next day announced that a British bomber had made a dastardly attack on Bardia the night before and set fire to and destroyed the hospital with great loss of life. The tummy was better the next day but the conscience pricked. I was consoled by thinking it was all a load of propaganda.

Then at the end of September, the Navy got very excited as a ship had been spotted in Bardia Harbour and we were alerted to try to sink it. Except when using up fuel for flare-dropping, Bardia was sufficiently close to the line for the attacks to be made from and return to Bagush but they still took over 3½ hours to complete. As we had a fullish moon, no flares were required on these occasions. The moon was bright enough to give me a feeling of nakedness up there. We carried a full bombload of two 500 and two 250 lb bombs on the first operation on 27th September. We were back at Bagush by 1 am on 28th September to rearm with six 250 lb bombs, have a cup of tea and out again, leaving the target area just before dawn. Then a third attack the following evening, this time with incendiaries in addition to six 250 pounders. On each occasion, the opposition was noticeably stronger. We lost a rear-gunner who died in the air after being hit by flak and there was a good deal of damage to aircraft. On the last attack, I saw an Me109 night fighter flash by, fortunately going in the opposite direction and up-moon. Seeing him gave me the shivers not least because we thought that the Luftwaffe did not indulge in night fighter sorties in the desert. However, here obviously was another hazard to be wary of.

We went on four days' leave next day and never have the beds at Dekheila felt so comfortable.

Mixed up with those attacks on Bardia were plenty of operations with a lot of variety. They were mainly army requested targets. The squadron were out most nights in varying numbers but I personally with my crew carried out three night reconnaissance raids looking for panzer concentrations though we always carried a bomb load in addition to flares in case we saw a likely target. There were also some ten attacks on such targets as stores dumps, and transport and tank concentrations. In these cases the army usually gave us a grid reference to make for. Judging by their reaction, the army were always grateful for any information we could bring back. These forays took place in the square from Ras el Milh, the point north of Bardia, south to Sidi Omar on the Wire, and west as far as the Tobruk perimeter. We soon began to know every wadi, every track and every possible hiding place (if that is possible in the desert) for concentrations of tanks and transport.

And there was the obvious target of all – the airfields. These were perhaps the most rewarding as there were always plenty of aircraft, though, usually being dispersed, they were not always easy to hit. Nevertheless we were able to knock out a lot of them. Gambut, the Luftwaffe forward base, was a favourite. Reporters from the *Egyptian Mail* were always keen on a story. Returning to Dekheila after fairly intense operations, we were interviewed, resulting in the following report in next day's edition. An article in the *Egyptian Mail* mentions a raid in Gambut in the following words:

Raid on Gambut

Flying over Gambut in relays, naval aircraft recently dropped a stick of bombs right among some enemy aircraft at a dispersal point, setting two of them alight and probably damaging others.

'We were flying over the target at intervals,' said one naval pilot.

'There was a fair amount of flak coming up at us and one of our aircraft was held for a while in the light of two searchlights. One aircraft of the flight before mine dropped a stick of bombs which fell right among some enemy aircraft. When we came along we could see two bright fires burning where the aircraft had been standing.'

We also visited the two airfields at Gazala, called Gazala North and South; Tmimi and Derna landing grounds were also on the agenda. Apart from Gambut, they were all long hauls entailing starting from Sidi Barrani and landing back there for refuelling.

It was at Tmimi that I first learnt how to deal with searchlights. It was an eerie feeling being caught by one. One minute, one was in darkness, then suddenly caught in the beam like someone turning on the light in the bedroom at dead of night. The answer, I found, in order to prevent being thrown off course, was to waggle the wings fairly violently. The searchlight crew followed the suspected turn and once they had lost you, they started groping round the sky to no effect. A game of blind man's bluff.

Then, on 2nd November, I took part in the first of the Pathfinder operations. Up to that time we had illuminated the target with our flares, or on a big raid with two specialist Albacore flare droppers. That night we found the target which were stores dumps south of the Bardia to Tobruk road and west of Gambut. We then illuminated the target for Blenheims of the RAF to attack by means of high level bombing. My log book adds the comment, 'Some good sticks but the target didn't give them much of a chance.' However, the great thing was that this was the first of such operations in which a squadron specializing in navigation had to find the target, and illuminate it for the bombers to attack it. It was the first of many such operations and undoubtedly led to the big Pathfinder operations over Germany by the RAF later in the war.

The idea was repeated two weeks later, this time cooperating with Wellingtons against Gazala South airfield. It was highly successful in spite of the presence of German night fighters in the shape of Me109's. The operation took place just before the big army push by Auchinleck and the Eighth Army and was a diversionary raid to cover an attack by paratroops on neighbouring airfields. Alas, the whole operation was compromised by a bombing aircraft forced-landing near Gazala.

The Eighth Army attack was timed for dawn on 18th November. We went up to Sidi Barrani for an attack on Tmimi airfield but it was cancelled. The note in my log book sums it up: 'What a night in a flooded tent. Electric and rain storms continued all night without abating. Whole desert a lake and every wadi a waterfall. Army push started at dawn.'

From then on to the end of January 1942, it was all go. First of all, for some reason, we switched refuelling airfields from Barrani to LG75 situated at the rail head further east of the line. I never did like LG75. Being surrounded by stores dumps it was under constant air attack both day and night. This meant running the gauntlet to land, sheltering in slit trenches till take off and then getting airborne as quickly as possible always hoping that a bomb or a crater didn't get you. I was always glad to get away from that place up into the safety of the air and the dark.

Then four days later, sadness struck. Returning from a raid on Tmimi, the log book note says that I 'landed with no oil temp or pressure. Oil tank found to be bone dry! The end of a very fine aircraft.' I had obviously come to love the old Albacore. I had flown this one constantly for four months. Lucky it wasn't the end of an aircrew too.

During the first seventeen days of December, I did nine night operations, most of them of over four hours' duration. You were held fast by parachute straps and safety harness and in no way could you move even a limb to relieve the stiffness that set in after a while. The parachute was a hard seat for the bum and eyes took the strain of peering into the darkness hour after hour. And the only thing to look forward to at the end of the op at an advance base was a cup of tea made with brackish water. Even that, however, tasted like nectar.

After the break-out by the Army and the Battle of Sidi Rezegh, the Germans were in full flight, so that targets were plentiful and easy to find. There was also plenty of variety in the targets. Attacks on tanks on the El Adem to El Duda road; MT concentrations near the Trigh Capuzzo and on the Bardia to Tobruk road the last attack on a suspected submarine at Bardia (the log book note says that the whole town was asleep for once!); more attacks on tanks west of El Adem; then we landed for refuelling at the forward landing ground at El Adem to take off later for two attacks on the airfield at Derna; and finally dive bombing convoys of lorries retreating west from Derna to Barce. On this occasion all the transport had their lights on, which made bombing simpler and highly successful.

Real tragedy struck, however, on our first visit to El Adem. This was quite a sophisticated airfield south of Tobruk. Mussolini had built it as a staging aerodrome during his Ethiopian campaign. It was of course new to us and we had no time to get accustomed to it as we landed for refuelling just before darkness fell. When all was ready, we prepared for take-off en route to bomb Derna airfield. We had all started up to take off in quick succession, the first to take off being Sub-Lieutenant Kyffin and his observer Lieutenant Harray. Imagine everyone's horror when we saw them making for the wrong end of the runway. They started taking off down wind, never made it and crashed into a building at the end and burst into flames. It seemed callous to continue the squadron take-off, especially as we had to start our run beside the burning wreck. Such is war. They were both a great loss to the squadron.

Just before Christmas, we began to move our desert base from Ma'aten Bagush to Bu Amud, a desolate bit of sand and not too

Captured Italian CR 42.

Ju88 at a captured desert airfield.

level, outside the Eastern part of the Tobruk perimeter on the Bardia
to Tobruk road. This was a distinct come-down after Bagush, like
a move from a good shack to poor shack. The squadron too tended
to get split up so that the corporate spirit disappeared. Apart from
Dekheila, units of the squadron would be dispersed at Bagush,
Barrani, Bu Amud and later Benghazi. Very rarely did we all get
together again until we were forced back to Dekheila when Rommel
arrived at El Alamein. We seemed to be shunted from airfield to
airfield according to the situation and with no settled home. The
squadron lost cohesion though that is not to say that we did not carry
out many and successful operations during this period. We lost a
home but gained the advantages of variety in our new nomadic
existence.

One unexpected gain did emerge from this wandering
commission which naturally arose from the rapid advance by the
Army. Often we would land at a new forward airfield which had
been hurriedly evacuated by the Germans or Italians earlier in the
day. The quicker the move, the more stores and equipment tended
to be left behind. We would find whole planes with only minor
defects preventing them from being flown, together with useful hauls
of spares. Jackets and other clothing would be plentiful as were the
Jerry-cans but the prize of all were the German cameras. Sometimes
these had a half-used film inside which produced some very
interesting photographs taken from the German or Italian angle.
But there was a casualty too. 'Body' Corpes, one of the squadron's
experienced observers, was using an enemy rifle one day when it
backfired on him resulting in his sadly losing the use of one of his
eyes.

Our first two attacks from Bu Amud were highly successful. The
first, when we carried six 250 lb bombs, gave us a perfect target of
some thirty closely parked large aircraft at Derna landing ground.
With no opposition from ack-ack, we had no difficulty in placing the
stick of bombs right among them. Alas, the other half of the
squadron flying that night were told to go to Barce but they couldn't
find the place! A bit of a waste with all those aircraft at Derna
waiting to be put out of action. Finally on 18th December 1941 we
attacked the retreating Italians on the Derna to Barce road. The
road was packed with lorries often two or three abreast and all with

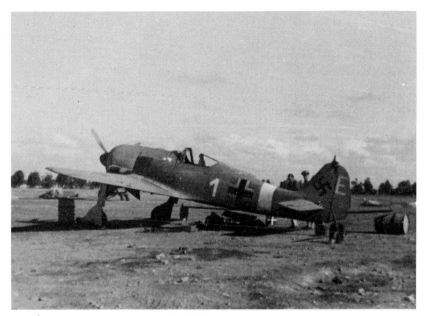

FW190 at Benghazi

German troops in the desert – from film in captured camera.

Ju52 with German parachutists before attack on Crete – from film in captured German camera.

German parachutists drop on Crete – from film in captured German camera.

German officer and U-boat at Bardia – from film in captured German camera.

German officer in Libya – from film in captured German camera.

their lights on. There was no difficulty in causing a traffic jam that night. We landed back at an emergency forward airfield after the raid. It was none other than Gazala South which I had seen from the air and bombed on many a night when it was occupied by the Italian and German airforces. After parking the plane, we went to the makeshift mess in a wooden shack for a cup of brackish tea and whom should I run into but my instructor from Netheravon days, Flight Lieutenant Ievers, with whom I had flown from there to Cranwell on that hot but lovely Battle of Britain day eighteen months before. Every day after this until Christmas, was spent ferrying, all the way back to Dekheila, up again to Bu Amud, and back to Bagush.

There I was detailed to pick up a Polish General who had been in the desert inspecting his troops. Imperial General Zajac was to be flown back to Cairo. He was accompanied by his British aide, Captain Geddes. We had a good trip to Heliopolis outside Cairo where I left the grateful General and Geddes took me off to the Turf Club for lunch. Our outward appearance did not measure up to the quality of the Club or the food on offer. I felt like a tramp walking into Hurlingham. But in those days anyone who looked as if he had escaped from the desert was welcome in Cairo and Alex. And if you could say you had just come down from Gazala, better still.

The CO had the following letter of thanks from the General:

HQ POLISH FORCES
Middle East
9th January 1942

My dear Lt Commander Corbett

It is my very pleasant duty to convey you my sincere thanks for having given me the opportunity of a flight with an aeroplane of the Royal Navy.

At this occasion, please, accept as well as Sub. Lt. D.M. Judd, my cordial greetings and best wishes for the New Year.

Very sincerely yours

Zajac imp. gen.

I was lucky enough that my plane was due for a service and that went for me too. So, Christmas was spent in the comfort of Dekheila and luxury of the Sporting Club and the piss-ups in the flesh-pots of Alex.

The mess at Dekheila was clean, cool and spacious and the cabins or bedrooms were comfortably airy for sleeping. The Sudanese boys in their clean white full-length gowns and tarbooshes made good and loyal stewards. There was a pleasant lawn in front of the mess overlooking the sea for the cool lunchtime and evening drink. If there was work to do at the squadron we would spend the morning at the hangar, perhaps have a shut-eye in the afternoon and then repair into Alex by the six o'clock 'liberty boat' or bus for the evening's festivities. Otherwise, if not wanted on the station we would get into Alex early by bus or hitch-hiking. Buses arrived and left Alex at the Cecil Hotel in a central square just off the water front. We may have been irresponsible elsewhere in the city but we respected the Cecil. The management were always helpful and courteous to us. The food was quite good and the bar large and very reasonable in its prices. But the main attraction of the bar was our friend the ghullie-ghullie man. He would invariably appear soon after six and squat on the floor to do his magician tricks and practise his sleight of hand. He soon attracted an audience all round him to watch his magic and urge him on with further ackers. He was dressed in the local fashion of white pyjama-like suit from which he would pull out all sorts of cards and paraphernalia of the magician. His favourite one was to produce a dozen live chicks from nowhere. The show would last as long as ackers were thrown into his bag. He was good for the London Palladium any day.

We would shop in that wonderful street of shops Rue Saad Zaghoul in the centre of the city and lunch at the Union Bar, which produced the best French Onion soup I've ever tasted, followed by tea perhaps at Pastroudis. But most often we would make for the Sporting Club out of the city to the east. That was a fine and popular haven. Facilities for tennis, golf and squash were laid on every day and the pool was well equipped. We were given temporary membership for next to nothing and had the run of the place. A special feature of the Sporting Club was the magnificent sticky cake tea in the spacious lounge. Daughters of local merchants, all very

Richard Hayes, 'Tatts' Tattersall, and Edgar Russell at the Sporting Club in Alex.

'Tatts' Tattersall, Edgar Russell and Ossie Lloyd at the Sporting Club in Alex.

wealthy and many of European descent, would be allowed to come to the club between 4 and 6.30 without chaperones and could join us for tea. They certainly added glamour, beauty and wealth to the scene.

Then back to town for the evening. Apart from many squalid and tawdry places of highly doubtful reputation, Alex had some four or five good night spots for drinking, dining and dancing. The Excelsior which had a summer and winter place and the Carlton on the Corniche were the favourites. The families of wealthy local merchants and Egyptians frequented them and we were allowed to dance with their daughters provided we returned them to their family table at the end of the dance! Those who did not choose to look for further entertainment met at the Cecil for the 11.30 bus the worse for an evening on horse's necks at the equivalent of 3p a time.

The plane serviced again, I took off for Bu Amud early in the new year. Three and a half hours of hard slog up the desert in the heat of the day was no fun. I was looking forward to that cup of tea after landing but before I could park the plane, Edgar Russell who was then in charge at Bu Amud came running out, climbed up the wing and shouted above the noise of the engine, 'You've got to take off again after refuelling, with a torpedo and stores, for Benghazi – there may be a torpedo attack tonight.'

I was hot and exhausted and the idea of taking off again almost immediately to fly over country I didn't know and land at Berka, one of the three or four airfields at Benghazi, at night where I hadn't been before, filled me with horror. And I would have no observer as I was to take up two groundcrew. So we took off from Bu Amud together with torpedo and stores just before sunset and made west.

I was to cross the Jebel Akhdar, a range of green mountains rising to some 3,000 feet between Derna and Benghazi. So for safety's sake I climbed to 7,000 feet after passing Gazala and flew on in the dark and dismal night. I flew first south-west hoping to spot Benghazi in due time. But the wind had got up to some strength from the south and my ground speed fully laden was slow in the extreme. My speed in the air was not much more than ninety knots so that over the ground I was doing about 50 knots! Nothing appeared, although by now I should be expecting to see the coast at Benghazi. No observer to consult and I began to get the feeling that I was completely and utterly lost. I examined all the options open to me. But there was really only one and that was to keep going west provided my compass was accurate and provided I hadn't been blown off course to the north and would now be making for Italy. Just as I was beginning to feel symptoms of panic I spotted the thin white line of the coast – but I was perilously near the tip of the coast where it turns from a westerly direction to a southerly one. So I turned to a southerly course for Benghazi. Shortly the town came into view, but where would I find Berka airfield? I came down to 1,500 feet and circled inland from Benghazi. And suddenly four very faint pinpoints of light appeared in a straight line. It must be Berka; and I knew so when the lights followed me round the circuit. The landing was successful thanks to the high wind but I counted myself lucky when I found out afterwards that the flair path consisted of four hand torches. I was glad to step down to firm ground. It was not a very happy night flight.

All this to no avail as the torpedo attack had already been cancelled. So the next day, we about turned for Dekheila via Bu Amud. The first part of that flight had its moments too. The wind of the previous night had whipped up a sandstorm so we flew back following a course south of the mountains. We landed at Msus airfield for lunch. This had obviously been an Italian airfield as the officers' mess had enough Chianti to stock a Naples bar for a week. We took advantage of this ill-gotten gain. It went down well with bully beef sandwiches. But too much Chianti had delayed our start and by then the sandstorm was beginning to intensify. It was a hairy flight at a hundred feet following the track to Mechili and Gazala and then along the beach, past Tobruk to Bu Amud. I was thankful to be back with a mixture of sand in the eyes and mouth and too much Chianti in the stomach, feeling, as a result, bloody awful.

After the attack at Benghazi and return, we had to get back to Dekheila for another service of the plane which turned out in the end to mean a new one. But, combined with this was one of those unplanned, unexpected parties which are always the best. Our visit to Dekheila coincided with one by Johnny Brown and his crew and it was his 21st birthday. Two other crews were there too. Now,

Johnny Brown was a laughing happy-go-lucky pilot from Wolverhampton with eternal optimism. He called himself 'Mrs Brown's favourite son'. There were all the makings of a huge binge known ever since as Johnny Brown's birthday party. It started in a small way at Dekheila, continued at the Sporting Club where plans were laid to meet at the Excelsior. Now, the Excelsior had a long oval bar. Cleared of bar paraphernalia, it resembled a race track. It wasn't long before the party thought so too. We were up on the bar at the signal and thanks to the brandy on board were soon chasing round it sending all the trappings flying and pulling down all the overhead electric wiring. The local diners panicked and left to a man falling over tables and chairs in the rush in the darkened room for the exit doors.

Having done our damnedest to turn the management against all things British for life, we all left for another nighterie and a third leaving behind equal pandemonium. The last port of call was the Carlton which had been tipped off by the other three places, 'Look out, they are coming.' But this didn't prevent Johnny Brown carrying one of the potted palms into the middle of the dance floor and dropping it; and Bobby Bradshaw raiding the kitchen for eggs and after removing the waiters' tarbooshes, cracking the eggs over their heads. At the time it was the party of all parties, but forty years on, it seems to be a disgraceful exhibition by irresponsible youths.

The law caught up with us at the Anglo-Hellenic Club where the Provost Marshal – a Major Royal Marines – took our names for the Commander's report the next day.

We duly lined up before the Commander of Dekheila at 10.30 next morning.

'Disgraceful behaviour ... disgusting ... a poor advertisement ... and 14 days confined to the station.' But we were all going up to the desert next day! We repaired to the bar to sort out the appalling hangovers when later the Commander came over to Johnny Brown and said, 'Why the hell didn't you let me in on that party, but for God's sake don't do it again.' We also remained on good terms with our friends, the restaurant managers. I didn't see any falling off of trade next time we were down in Alex, nor were we refused entry.

With the new plane that was to see me through until July, we had another dash to Benghazi for a torpedo attack on a large troop convoy supported by the Italian fleet bound for Tripoli. We flew up to Bu Amud from Dekheila on 22nd January, then on to Berka Satellite airfield the next day. That was the day that Rommel unexpectedly started his advance from Agedabia towards Benghazi and all points east. Berka was a shambles by the time we arrived. The RAF were to carry out daylight attacks on the convoy followed by 826 Squadron's Albacores. Reports of the movement of the convoy kept coming in. It appeared we had little time in which to refuel and get out to the Gulf of Sirte for the attack before the convoy turning west for Tripoli went out of range. Refuelling was from petrol drums and the Albacores were the last in the queue. Jack Corbett took off with the first flight leaving the last three to follow, including us, and led by Bobbie Bradshaw. Delay followed delay, and by the time we took off, we had little chance of finding the convoy. We therefore rather lamely returned to Berka after a fruitless search in the dark.

However, the attack was not altogether a failure; Ferret Ellis hit the large Italian troopship *Victoria* (later sunk by the FAA squadron of Swordfish based on Malta) and Johnny Brown hit a destroyer. Our CO, Jack Corbett, was, alas, shot down though fortunately he and his crew, Jacko Jackson and Bugden, were picked up by the Italians. Next day we had to evacuate Berka and return to Bu Amud, exhausted, frustrated and saddened (not knowing whether or not Jack Corbett had survived but fearing the worst). This was followed by two nights of intense activity when we flew to Tmimi to refuel in order to dive bomb tank and MT concentrations at Msus where we had been wining and dining off Chianti and bully beef less than three weeks before.

During this last week of January our new CO, Lieutenant Smith, joined us in the middle of a sandstorm at Bu Amud. Sadly, he only lasted a few weeks. When we had retreated back to Bagush satellite, he took off one day for Dekheila with a plane load of 'liberty men' bound for Alex when he was jumped by a Ju88 and shot down. There were no survivors. He was followed as CO by Paul Compton.

February 1942 was a dismal month. We soon had to evacuate Bu Amud ahead of Rommel's advance to the Bir Hacheim-Gazala line.

Phil Wise taking over 'R' for Robert in July 1942.

Brian Cooper and Bobby Bradshaw in the desert.

For the rest of the month based at our original desert airfield of Ma'aten Bagush satellite, we were relegated to anti-submarine patrols between there and Sidi Barrani. On only one occasion did we see a U-boat. Unfortunately, he beat me in our respective crash dives and I could only depth charge where I thought he might be. But no tell-tale debris appeared and I could only hope that I might have shaken him.

The month did redeem itself toward the end when we carrried out our second flare-dropping sortie for Wellingtons. This entailed a three and a half hour flight from Dekheila to Sidi Aseiz to refuel followed by a long night flight to Martuba airfields near Derna and back lasting five and a half hours. But it was a very successful attack. We were able to illuminate plenty of parked aircraft and the Wellingtons made good use of the plentiful targets.

The unforeseen was always lurking round the corner and drama was never far away in those desert days and nights. Somehow, one felt very naked up there above the flat desert or the sea, chugging along at 95 knots, less if bombs, flares and a torpedo were being carried. No hiding place, rarely a cloud in which to take refuge and no speed above 100 knots to get you out of trouble. The darkness of the night was a relief to the nerves but there was no escaping the glare and clarity of a desert day. One prayed that one would not come face to face with an enemy fighter. The bookies wouldn't have given us any odds. What chance had an Albacore in such circumstances?

It happened, though, out of the blue on the morning of 10th March 1942.

Rommel had by then halted his advance from Agedabia on the line between Bir Hacheim and Gazala. Although the squadron had evacuated Bu Amud, it was felt that the airfield could be operated by a flight of no more than three planes which were relieved every week or so. On this day, it was my turn to lead a relief flight to Bu Amud from which we would be able to carry out night dive bombing attacks on enemy airfields and tank concentrations with only about half-an-hour approach flight. Dickie Nathan and Stevens were to pilot the other two planes. We were to carry a full load of six 250 lb bombs, flares slung underneath and stores packed into the rear cockpit beside Denis McIntosh and our air-gunner, Leading

Aircraftman Harper. We knew the area so well that detailed briefing was unnecessary. The only briefing I got, ironically as it turned out, was to by-pass the Sidi Barrani/Sollum area as German fighters were known to patrol there. We decided to fly at 100 feet and in extended line abreast. We took off from Ma'aten Bagush and set course along the coast until we were just short of Barrani where we would swing inland towards the railhead, across the Wire near Fort Maddelena and then swing back towards the coast at Gambut to make Bu Amud.

It was one of those perfect desert days – a cloudless sky, hot and clear and the desert below stretching out in all its strange beauty. Near the railhead we had been joined by an RAF Wellington overtaking us about a mile to our left. Then I spotted an aircraft flying across and behind us in the left quarter. I called to Mac down the voice pipe:

'Mac, there's an aircraft on the port quarter!'

'Yes,' he said in his usual calm way. 'One of ours, I think.'

I felt relieved but feeling also that he had no more knowledge of the identity of the aeroplane than I had. In the next second all was starkly revealed as this interloper into the desert peace began to attack the Wellington. Seconds later the bomber crashed and burst into flames.

'That's a Messerschmitt, Mac,' I shouted, trying to hide the rising panic in my voice. 'And, look, there are two of them.'

Everything stopped still at that moment and I froze at the sight of the fighters. We were sitting ducks for the 109s – a real piece of cake for them.

Then the fun started. Dicky Nathan, on my left, was shot down and crash landed and was being shot up on the ground. Now it was our turn. I felt shit-scared beyond belief and almost incapable of thoughts or action. Like one of those heavy slow Wildebeasts with a lion on its tail about to jump. But it was no good running away; the only chance of survival in a slow aircraft being attacked by a fast fighter was to keep turning inside him. But could I get into a tight steep turn and not stall, with the load I was carrying. There was no alternative.

'Mac,' I shouted, 'tell me when they come within range.'

The next moment, Mac started his commentary in a steady voice and without panic. 'They are turning into us from the port quarter now ... they are straightening up ... wait for it ... they are coming in ... Turn ... Now.'

Hard port rudder and stick jammed over to the left and then hard back into my stomach. What a sluggish old crate this is, I thought, bombs and all. But nothing hit us and the next second the MEs appeared in front of me. They had missed; I felt we weren't beaten yet; but they would be attacking us again, that was for sure.

Mac started talking again: 'Starboard quarter ... attack coming ...' and he gave me the same clear directions.

It is at moments like this that the back tenses, everything in the body tenses and the feeling of being shot in the back is the most acute. And you can't see what is happening. Certainly, Mac was superb in all his talk-down but with split seconds involved, it feels better to see what is happening. The waiting between the beginning of an attack and the turn into the circle was like eternity though only in fact a second or two. The MEs would have been closing at about 300 mph and to them this was a real cinch – an Albacore in their sights flying straight and level at 90 mph. A bit of shooting practice but with three guys at the receiving end.

Mac shouting 'Turn ... now' galvanized me into action. Kick rudder hard to starboard and stick over and back till the old machine groaned into a steep turn and the desert spun round. Then I thought of the bombs – did they explode on being hit by bullets or cannon shells? Oh! Christ, isn't this enough?

This time they were more successful. Hits were scored in the rear cockpit and a cannon shell came through to hit the instrument panel on my left – just beside me. Too near – a bloody unfair contest, I thought. I would have had the feeling of giving up at this point except that the stakes were too high. I had no time to freeze or to panic as the next and port attack followed quickly. There were more hits on us but miraculously the propeller kept going round and the controls still answered to the touch.

I remember on this occasion looking out the port side of the cockpit at the sand below. I saw a service man walking across the desert below us towards the railhead. He was looking up at the dog fight 100 feet above him. Could I hear him say, 'Poor buggers'?

Now came a lull. It seemed a long time and Mac wasn't talking, but it was probably only seconds. I was looking round the cockpit at the damage. No blood, no pain but a mess where the cannon shell had exploded. Then something made me look up and there it was head on and closing at maximum speed. It was an instant reaction to avoid a crash that made me jam the stick forward and just hope. It was just that hundredth of a second in time. The ME had us in his sights but he left it too late. The bullets and shells went over the cockpit and hit the tail plane.

I was beginning to shake and felt sure that our luck couldn't last. Nor, I thought, would my nerves. Where was the next attack coming from and how many would there be and how long was all this hell going to last? Then to my amazement and relief, they appeared in front and just above me, flying away in formation to their base. Probably running short of fuel or out of ammunition. I would never know but it didn't matter – they were gone, two disappointed Messerschmitt pilots going home to lunch.

It was not however, all one way shooting. Our rear-gunner, Leading Aircraftman Harper, had been busy firing away at them with his twin Vickers K guns in his rear cockpit as the enemy attacked. He believed he had hit them.

It was clearly no good going on to Bu Amud. The only safe thing to do was to land as quickly as possible. Sidi Barrani was the nearest airfield. We first made for the sea and climbed for height to drop the bombs and then landed – or crash landed – with burst tyres. We climbed out unhurt but shaking, our legs feeling like jelly and with all sorts of jumbled up emotions, not least those of relief, thankfulness and on top of it all, a strange kind of elation.

The old crate, much maligned, was not so bad after all. It seemed to stand there in the desert that morning proud that though it was bent, it was not broken.

Fortunately Albacore No 8979, which I had been flying since January, was capable of repair, though it took three weeks at Dekheila to make her fit for flying again. She stayed with me till I left the squadron in July but this incident was to turn out to be the first of three hair-raising escapes.

We were able to rejoin the squadron at Ma'aten Bagush satellite at the beginning of April and our first operation was a highly successful Pathfinder sortie for the Wellingtons against Martuba

(Left) Over Bu Amud (Note Tobruk in top left of photograph). *(Right)* At Sidi Barrani after the scrap with the Me109s.

Bill Orwin and Bobby Bradshaw near Benghazi.

airfield near Derna, a return flight of five hours. But the situation
at the front was getting dangerous and Rommel was expected to
launch an attack against Tobruk shortly. It was therefore deemed
advisable to bring the forward arm of the squadron back to Dekheila
in the middle of April. There were also signs that the Italian fleet
would put to sea in support of Rommel's push forward. We therefore
embarked on some intensive torpedo attack practice off Dekheila.

These were carried out by all available aircraft in the squadron
climbing to about 10,000 feet in formation, then opening out to dive
for position to turn into the attack at 50 – 100 feet above the sea, the
target usually being a destroyer of the fleet based in Alexandria
harbour. After several daylight attacks, we turned to a night attack
and it was on this occasion that the second mishap occurred. We had
formed up after take off from Dekheila and were making out to the
target area, climbing steeply. At about 3,000 feet my engine began
to cough and splutter but in spite of attempted remedial action, the
engine still sounded rough and ominously failing. I could only fall
out of the formation and make for home. It became clear as I made
for the coast some twenty miles away that I might not make
Dekheila. In fact the engine was very nearly stopped by the time I
saw the coast. Very luckily, it was a moonlight night. But where
should I land? In the sea, if I hadn't made land in time though this
was not to be recommended with the Albacore's fixed
undercarriage. The desert was not desirable thereabouts either.
There were plenty of dunes and soft sand which would mean
finishing up on our back. How about the beach, I thought? Shall I
make it?

I did my best to coax the engine along but it was clear by now
that if I did make the beach, I couldn't look at it first and choose
the best spot. In particular I had no idea whether the beach was
shallow or steep. Anyway, beggars can't be choosers, so 'Landing
on beach, Mac, turning into landing approach now.'

The moonlight showed up a lonely white sandy beach, but was
it soft or hard. Can't do anything about it, here goes. We dropped
down almost engine-less. The wheels touched, the tail touched, and
she ran along the sandy beach as faultlessly as if it was a hard
runway. The engine gave up the ghost as we came to rest. Otherwise
there was no damage to the aircraft and we got out very relieved and

Albacores over the desert.

Albacores at Sidi Barrani.

glad to be safe. We waited a long time hoping that news of our defection had reached them but not a soul came near. The only thing to do was to walk over the sand to Dekheila which we reached in the small hours. A landing craft went out to collect the aircraft.

Leave was due and as this coincided with another crew, four of us, Peter Wellington, Tats Tattersall our Canadian, Mac and I spent a few days in Cairo. We stayed at Shepheards Hotel (this is the old Shepheards, now replaced by a new hotel elsewhere in the city). I remember our arrival. The hotel was reached by a stairway from the street, and then across a wide verandah running the length of the hotel. This verandah was packed that day with large, burly and well dressed Egyptians in black suits and fezs, all with the inevitable fly whisk. This turned out to be part of the convention being held in the hotel by the ruling WAFD party. Shepheards was an excellent hotel of its type; a colonial style and very spacious and comfortable – the Raffles of Cairo.

The centre of Cairo was as attractive as that of Alex with its broad streets, lovely shops and elegant buildings in the French style; the only difference was the crowds which were overpowering in Cairo. The streets seemed to be full of a seething mass of humanity almost round the clock. And like Alex, touts were everywhere hawking anything from filthy pictures to girls. Two or three of you would be walking along a busy street in the centre of either city at midday. You were all discussing where to go for a drink and good lunch when it became apparent that a small Arab urchin in filthy shorts and shirt and barefooted was buzzing around like a wasp around a jam jar. He was doing a recce on probable clientele. The conversation was opened by him and generally took the following form:

'You like girl, Master?'

'Buzz off.'

'I take you to nice girl, Master.'

'Oh! Go away.'

'I have sister, Master – very good, very clean.'

'Bugger off, I tell you.'

'My sister, very good, pink inside like Queen Victoria.'

'Oh for God's sake, fuck off.'

And so it would go on; he stuck with you like a leech. Nothing would shake him off till suddenly he would dart up an alley and was

Peter Wellington, 'Tatts' Tattersall, Denis McIntosh and the Author.

(Left) Peter Wellington, Edgar Russell, 'Doc' Duncan, Denis McIntosh, the Author and Richard Hayes outside the Cecil Hotel, Alex. (Right) Richard Hayes and the Author outside the Cecil Hotel, Alex.

gone. But there were hundreds of others to take his place.

The highlights of our visit were the mosque, the Pyramids of Gizeh and the Cairo Bazaar. I thought the Pyramids particularly fascinating especially the mathematical precision of the huge construction. We couldn't resist the invitation to go inside to see the Queen's Chamber though we had second thoughts by the time we got halfway up the steep slope to the centre where the King and Queen's chambers are situated. What a climb but at least it was cool underneath all that stone. It was pitch black in there too – even in the chambers. Our guide asked us if we would like to have a magnesium flare lit in the Queen's Chamber. That would cost us two ackers each every time. So we spent our ackers but saw little in the short duration of light except a square box-like room. But there was a wonderful mystery about it all.

Outside there were the obligatory camels to ride round the Pyramids and the Sphinx. There were only three left so that Peter Wellington had to content himself with a donkey. I made the unfortunate error of asking the minder of my camel whether he could gallop. The Arabic shout and crack of the whip and off we went. I was thrown up only to meet the camel's hump coming up as I was going down and this went on and on. The Arab was splitting his sides with laughter but wouldn't give the order to stop till he reckoned I had had my money's worth. Talk about sore arse!

We spent a hilarious morning in the Cairo bazaar especially as all the prices, even allowing for the expected bargaining, were outside our reach. The goods on show, mostly luxury items were out of this world. It was an Aladdin's Cave. At every shop we were pestered to go in and look. We eventually chose the *parfumerie*. As in every shop, we were treated like princes with large bank accounts. Seats were provided and coffee produced at regular intervals with chocolate and cigarettes. And what a display of perfumes. It was the long hard sell for the three or four shopkeepers. Perfume after perfume was produced and rubbed on the hands so that after a while the place began to smell like a whore's boudoir. In fact we were all willing to buy some for the girlfriend but as was expected of us, we were bargaining hard to the point where the owner was saying, 'But, Master I have a wife and family to keep' with tears welling up in his eyes.

Eventually we said we couldn't compete, got up and walked out. But we were pursued and urged to return. The prices had tumbled and we all bought our selected perfume at a tiny price compared with the starting offers. Honour was achieved on both sides and we parted the best of friends after a good morning's entertainment.

Back to Dekheila and a new engine had been fitted and X8979 was again raring to get into the fray. We were immediately involved nearly putting the torpedo practices to the test. We flew up to Bu Amud, landing there for the last time just before Rommel attacked on 26/27th February. After refuelling we flew on by night to the target area south west of Benghazi where there was supposed to be a convoy making for Benghazi with much needed supplies for the German Army. This was to be a Pathfinder mission with the roles reversed. Wellingtons with their superior equipment were to find the convoy and drop flares above it to guide us into the attack. Something went badly wrong in the Pathfinder force, and we never did see the convoy. Instead we had to carry our torpedoes back; a very long and tedious night flight.

Then soon after the German attack began at Gazala, we were off again on a torpedo attack, this time against the Italian Fleet which was supposed to be venturing out of Taranto to cover landings at Tobruk and to bombard the town but after an all night wait at Barrani for the 'off', we heard that the Fleet never left its port. In June there was another fruitless wait at Barrani; this time the Italian Fleet did sally forth but retired out of range.

Meantime the whole squadron carried out a very successful night minelaying operation in Derna harbour, a round trip of six hours. Part of Derna sits on the edge of high cliffs above the rest of the town and the harbour. The plan was to approach the harbour some five miles to the east at 50 feet, turning parallel to the coast under the cliffs to run in over the harbour to drop the mines between the two moles of the harbour. This operation called for great accuracy. This and the fact that we were in formation meant that the minimum of weaving or jinking could be carried out. All went well till we approached the harbour when all hell let loose as intense light anti-aircraft fire opened up from the shore. We were close enough to hear the guns and the shells. It was not a very pleasant few minutes and we were glad to get out of the area after dumping our mines in the harbour.

We were to return to Derna twice in two days at the beginning of June to dive bomb shipping in the harbour. Again the ack-ack was very accurate and intense including heavy guns firing at us during the approach and the dive. My logbook adds the note: 'For the first time Jerry heavy ack-ack seems to have an idea of firing at Albacores.' In previous operations heavy ack-ack shells invariably exploded well in front of us. Obviously the enemy thought they were firing at something a bit faster than 95 knots. I never counted them much of a menace.

The use of ack-ack and especially the light variety by the enemy at typical targets such as airfields was an interesting reflection of the national characteristics of the two countries fighting together on the opposite side. On approaching an enemy airfield at 8,000 feet, it was soon apparent who was defending it. If they were Italians, the airfield would erupt when you were a mile or two from the point of dive. The whole place would resemble a grand firework display with red, green and yellow traces shooting up into the sky in every direction without any reference to the position of the attacking planes. It added much colour and entertainment to the night's otherwise dull proceedings. Furthermore, the pyrotechnic display helped us by pinpointing exactly where the airfield was situated. The innocuous firing continued through the dive, the bombing and the pull away from the target.

If, however, you got near to the point of dive without the night air being disturbed in that way, it would be clear that the ack-ack guns were manned by Germans. They held their fire till the last minute and then opened up in a concerted attack when the bomber was committed to the dive. Their only fault was that they invariably aimed well in front of the Albacore, not appreciating that anything quite so slow could be abroad at night.

Tobruk surrendered to the German Army on 21st June. We flew up to Sidi Barrani on the 19th armed with mines ready to lay them in Tobruk harbour. For three days we were the most advanced flying unit in the desert, feeling very naked as rumour followed rumour of the German advancing columns. However, we were to evacuate this familiar and desolate spot in the desert, when we carried out two operations laying mines in Tobruk harbour on successive nights.

The first one was carried out while the British Army were still in possession but the Germans had taken over the town by the time we returned the next night. We were expecting a rough reception but received no opposition. It all felt rather eerie and sad. Later, on returning to Dekheila I was interviewed by John Nixon, Reuter's special correspondent with the Mediterranean Fleet, who wrote the following article in the *Egyptian Mail* under the headline:

PILOT SAW CLOUDS OF SMOKE IN TOBRUK

Alexandria, Wednesday

Tobruk was 'as quiet as a city of the dead', according to a young Naval pilot who flew there with others on two successive nights after the fortress fell.

'We met no opposition, either searchlights or anti-aircraft fire,' the pilot told me.

'The Germans must have seen us because there was a lot of moonlight – so much in fact that we could clearly make out tracks and buildings, and the boom across the harbour was most visible.

'It seemed almost as if there was nobody in the town.'

On the first night the pilots saw voluminous clouds of black smoke coming from a building on the quay, and, on both nights, passed a ship on fire some forty miles from Tobruk close to the shore. Big explosions were observed south-west of Tobruk on the horizon in the direction of Acroma.

'Our bombers must have been active as we saw flares being dropped and there was a lot of ack-ack fire going up,' the pilot added.

'The quiet Tobruk itself was almost uncanny. Altogether it was a very pleasant trip both nights.'

All the pilots got back safely.

During the present fighting the Naval Air Service has been helping by countering submarines, guarding convoys, and assisting in bombing enemy transport columns and tank concentrations. Naval aircraft fly over the transport columns and tanks, and drop flares to mark them for the bombers, which follow on. For this work they have been specially congratulated by Air Headquarters, Western Desert. – Reuter.

The German advance was so quick that by 25th June we were flying from Bagush for the last time in a flare-dropping operation for Wellingtons on enemy mobile columns at Barrani. The next night we carried out our bombing of MT units at Barrani, doing a lot of damage. Later that day we evacuated Bagush for Daba. That afternoon enemy fighters were patrolling over Bagush and Bobby Bradshaw and Edgar Russell had lucky escapes when they were shot up there. By the 28th we were bombing MT near Mersa Matruh after which we returned direct to Dekheila. On 30th June and 1st July we attacked Fuka airfield where we caused plenty of damage to Ju52's parked there.

So the squadron was now all back at Dekheila almost a year after we had originally set out into the desert. We were all disenchanted and disheartened and the squadron was in disarray. We had set out a year before with high hopes that our close support would continue as we followed the advance begun by the Army in November 1941 and that we would end up in Tripoli as part of the effort to throw the enemy out of North Africa. But it wasn't to be. We got as far as Benghazi but were only able to stay there for some three weeks before Rommel took advantage of a weak desert army to turn an armed reconnaissance into a full blooded push to Bir Hacheim/Gazala. From then on we were on the retreat, often operating at night and evacuating airfields in the daytime all the way back to Alex. We felt sad and demoralised. It seemed that all the effort and danger had been for nothing. We were still on retreat after nearly three years of war and we were up against a seemingly unbeatable machine in the German Afrika Korps, brilliantly led by Rommel who had superior equipment at his disposal.

Events were to prove that this was the Allies' nadir. The German advance had been so quick and decisive that there seemed to be no reason why Rommel shouldn't continue for the next forty miles to Alex which would give him virtually the Nile Delta and therefore the whole of Egypt. The rest of the Near East would have then been at his command. But fate was to decide otherwise. The German advance had been too quick and they had a long supply line. Petrol was short as were tanks and guns. Furthermore the Allies had made a stand at Alamein where the passable route becomes a bottleneck between the coast and the Qattara Depression. Rommel could not use his favourite ploy of out-flanking his enemy.

None of this was generally known at the end of June and during the first day or so of July. Everyone expected the next forty miles to be rolled up by the Germans as easily as the previous 300 miles. The fleet had left Alex to a point south of the Canal as soon as Tobruk had surrendered, as it would have been vulnerable to air attacks in the harbour. The effect of this on morale was immense. Alex harbour was empty and the city itself dead. The decision gave the impression of panic and retreat however logical it may have been from a military point of view. We asked where we should be going when Dekheila came to be evacuated. We were told semi-officially that we might be flying off east to Iraq or Persia ... but on the other hand we might be ordered to Kenya. The mind boggled not only at the impending disaster for the Allies but the sheer endurance test of such flights. I say that the word was semi-official because no one knew. Chaos reigned. And anyway, who would be caring for 826 Squadron in such a situation?

Fortunately, the mood didn't last. It became increasingly clear that the Germans had been halted. Further, we were kept busy. The new mood and the operations that we were called upon to undertake was summed up well in an article in the *Egyptian Mail* by Edwin Tetlow of the *Daily Mail* in which he said:

'The Desert's Flying Sailors Are Shy Young Men'

Nothing much has been heard so far in this war about the young men who are working hard against Rommel from one of the Royal Navy's most remarkable and most belligerent outposts on the coast of North Africa.

They are flyers in the Naval Air Service or Fleet Air Arm if you like. They belong to the desert's shyest striking force.

If it weren't for an occasional brief communique we would never know that they existed.

But the enemy knows they are there all right. You have to take a car from Alexandria and drive from civilisation to sandy

826 Squadron at Dekheila – August 1942.

desolation to reach them.

You have to pass through strong points manned by sailor sentries who keep constant watch lest some enemy visitors by sea or air should try to enter this stronghold which is doing them so much hurt. Once past the guards you are in a strange place indeed. It is an aerodrome which is run exactly as if it were an aircraft-carrier, which never goes to sea.

The white ensign flies from its 'masthead' – its name is not Flying Station such and such, but HMS G...

You are said to go aboard when you enter its sandy confines and to go ashore by liberty boat when you take taxi or car to drive to Alexandria.

You eat in Wardroom, not mess, with Sub-Lieutenants and other officers who dress in naval uniform and who are only to be distinguished from their sea-going comrades by a letter 'A' (meaning air) in loop of their rings of rank on their tunic sleeves.

They call their bedrooms cabins and there is even a bosun to carry out the orthodox naval duties as the link between this aerodrome's – sorry, I mean ship's – complement of ratings and officers.

Every evening they lower the colours at sunset in full accord with naval tradition. All these facts show that the Royal Navy is making sure its youngest offshoot shall not lose any of its naval flavour, although its destiny is not to be on the sea, but in the air.

This tender schooling will have important consequences as inevitably the Naval air component grows in size and importance in the years to come.

I have spent the night with the desert's flying sailors. We dined and chatted together – chiefly about home of course – and then company in the wardroom dwindled as the night became older and in twos and threes the flyers went to put on old sweaters and mufflers over their uniforms and prepare to take off. We could hear them roaring off at regular intervals over the wardroom roof on a variety of missions. There seemed indeed every kind of mission to be done that night. The Navy's planes are maids-of-all-work.

On this quite normal night they were going out to look for submarines and to torpedo enemy shipping carrying supplies to Rommel, to reconnoitre the desert, to drop flares for their big bombing brothers of the R.A.F., to seek out targets for themselves along El Alamein line – and to do their own dive-bombing.

The commander, although still young, has had a long career at sea, but in the last few years he has specialised in flying. He has an avuncular interest in each rating and officer working with him. He warned me, as we walked through the black-out to the wooden 'Ops' hut, not to expect glowing tales from the men who were coming back.

'If there's one thing they're afraid of – and it is about the only thing – it's being suspected of shooting a line,' he said. So it proved. These I saw on their return had been on aggressive reconnaissance patrols over Rommel's lines.

Their instructions had been to stooge around persistently until they found their special targets and then to dive-bomb.

To listen as they gave their unexciting answers to questions by the intelligence officer as they lounged around the map-covered table in the hut, one might have thought they had been out on practice flights instead of the dangerous and thrilling sorties over the heart of the enemy's concentrations in the desert.

'Yes, we saw a good number of German tanks moving about at the southern end of El Alamein line,' said one bearded boy as he puffed at a welcome cigarette.

'We picked out some lorries for ourselves – just there. We had a bit of flak but not much. We dived pretty low and then let go.' The intelligence officer asked him if he thought their bombs had scored any hits. ' Well ... er ... don't want to shoot a line, but, as a matter of fact, they did,' was the embarrassed answer. Other crews were just as modest.

The only flyer who really was voluble, was one navigator, an ex-bank clerk in the Midlands, and that was not on account of what he and his fellow members of the squadron had done, but in praise of the work done by the RAF planes which had also been out that night.

'Were those Wellingtons doing a good job of work,' he said with eyes sparkling. 'They gave Jerry's tanks a real dosing. I saw one tank go up in the loveliest explosion I've ever seen out here.'

After they had made their reports, the crews went to the wardroom for 3.00 am bacon, eggs and tea. Then some went back towards the airfield. 'Where are they going?' I asked. 'Oh, they're going out on patrol again,' I was told. 'They often do that. There's a lot to do these nights.'

Think proudly then, of these flying sailors and their aircraft-carrier aerodrome in the desert the next time you read in the Middle East communique that, '... The RAF, assisted by naval aircraft has done this or that.'

Bear in mind, that they were the first to spot Rommel's earliest moves preceding his recent profitless attack, that it was they who played havoc with the barges and lighters in Mersa Matruh harbour, that it is they who are smashing into the Eastern Mediterranean – but there, that's shooting a line, and they don't like that.

After five sorties in five nights, we were involved in an all night blitz on MT dispersed at Alamein. In the first sortie we provided illumination for Wellingtons and then joined in with bombing runs of our own, using the front and rear guns to add to the many fires that were burning. The concentrations of MT were such that you couldn't miss. Back to Dekheila to refuel and rearm and off again.

It is said that everything runs in threes. For me there had been two up to now and there was one to go. And it happened to me that night, taking off for the second time bound for Alamein. It was then that the girfriend, X8979, and I parted company for good. Whether it was she or I who got tired of the relationship, I'll never know. Perhaps it was by mutual consent. It had been a long and happy, if at times stormy, affair. I somehow lost the end of the runway lights, hit a store, bounced off the wall at the end of the runway. At this point, the coast which formed a T with the operating runway turned 90° to the right so that an extending line of the runway would run parallel to the coast. Some hundred yards along this stretch of shore was the officers' mess. The engine cut out over the coast and ditching was inevitable.

In those few seconds, I wondered whether at stalling speed I could get the tail down to prevent a somersault on hitting the water and secondly whether the bombs with sticks on them would go off. The answers soon manifested themselves; I did and they didn't. Ironically I landed just opposite the mess some thirty yards out. We had only one thought; to get out quick in case anything happened to the bombs or fuel and we set off to swim to shore as fast as we could. We were met by a cheering mob of officers. What an undignified way of entering the mess! I was met by the squadron doctor who diagnosed shock and grounded me indefinitely. I left the squadron to recuperate and for reposting to the UK. So ended what turned out to be a truly memorable year with all the fear and danger, the companionship and fun with so many friends in 826 Squadron.

The girl friend lived on to serve the mess for some time. We had landed in shallow water so that the upper plane was two or so feet above the surface, making an ideal diving board.

I joined the staff of the CO Naval Air Station at Dekheila and got back to flying towards the end of August. While waiting for a flight back to UK, I kept my hand in with ferry and aircraft testing trips together with an interesting trip by air to Haifa, Beirut, Rayack, a free French airfield between Damascus and Baalbeck, and Gaza.

At that time, about the only way of flying home was the infrequent service from Cairo to Lagos, then to Lisbon and home. A landing at neutral Lisbon involved travelling in civilian clothes, with a passport stating that the holder was a Government employee. I was all set to travel this way when an RAF Halifax arrived from the UK with urgent medical supplies. It was returning immediately. I was lucky to cadge a lift. The aircraft crewed by Czechs was normally used to drop men by parachute into occupied France. It was not therefore the most comfortable of aircraft in the back. However, it only took four days, which was a consolation.

We took off from Cairo to Malta. The weather was fine there but by the time we flew over Benghazi at dusk, the clouds looked threatening and the weather deteriorated fast. Soon, the pilot, Flight Lieutenant Kroll, came back to say that he had just received a signal from Luqa that the weather there had closed in and he was to return to Cairo. The determined captain had only one thought – to get back to the UK as quickly as possible. He told me and my three companions in very good English that he was going to ignore the signal, had not received it if asked, would press on to Malta regardless and requested us to feign ignorance. We were forced down to sea level under black cloud and in heavy rain by the time we made Malta. Luqa had picked us up on their set and had put on the searchlights to guide us in. Kroll had to climb over the cliffs and flop down on the runway at Luqa.

A lovely piece of flying. But trouble awaited him. As we got out of the Halifax, a car drew up with the Station Wing Commander.

'What the hell are you doing landing here in these conditions. We had to put on the searchlights for you which is about the easiest way of telling enemy planes where we are. Didn't you get my signal?'

Kroll replied in very broken English, 'No, Sir, no signal.'

The Wing Commander turned to us appealing to the Englishman's sense of honesty but we didn't let our gallant captain down. The Wing Commander departed utterly disbelieving.

The storm cleared after two days. As we were preparing for take-off we heard that the plane ahead of us also bound for the UK had crashed on take-off with no survivors. However, we made Gibraltar without further incident. Next day, the wide sweep around the Bay of Biscay and a flight up to Tempsford from the land fall at Land's End. How good it was to see the green fields again after twenty months away. I had forgotten how lovely England is.

But our captain had the last word. He came aft to tell us that he had received a signal to land at Hern for customs clearance. No way would he comply and he was making for home base.

I was soon home for Christmas and three weeks' leave.

CHAPTER EIGHT

Interlude

I received my new posting just before Christmas. It was to be a complete change of scene, a new project, a change of style, a challenge. I was appointed to a brand new squadron – No 845 Naval Air Squadron. We were to go to the United States to form up the new squadron on the fairly recently designed Avenger made by Grumman. Although one Naval Air Squadron – No 832 – had been converted to Avengers the previous year to serve in HMS *Victorious* which was lent to the Americans for service in the South Pacific in 1943, 845 was to be the first of a long line of Avenger squadrons. We were therefore breaking new ground to be followed month by month by other new Avenger squadrons.

The Avenger had first seen operations flying at the Battle of Midway in June 1942. It was a three-seater strike aircraft capable of carrying one torpedo or four 500 lb bombs in an enclosed bomb-bay. Its performance appeared to be distinctly more up-to-date than the slow, heavy and pedestrian Albacore. I had formed a great affection for the Albacore after a long partnership together, but the prospect was exciting as I was making for the States to fly a new aircraft and one that was, according to the reports, made for the job of a carrier-based strike aircraft. Furthermore, I had been promoted to Lieutenant. That would mean I would have a flight in the new squadron and would be able to leave behind the role of arse-end Charlie. If nothing else, the pay was marginally better!

I was to report to Lee-on-Solent at the beginning of January 1943. The nucleus of the squadron's aircrew and the ground crews foregathered there before leaving for the States where we would make up the numbers by taking in new aircrew newly trained at American Service flying schools such as Pensicola and Fort Lauderdale. We were all new to each other and the first few days were spent shooting lines about past experiences, speculating about the future and getting to know each other. We had for those days a larger than normal RN element, for by 1943 RNVR officers were beginning to take over flying appointments in squadrons from the CO downwards. Lieutenant-Commander 'Wilf' Crawford RN was the CO. Lieutenant Johnny Johnson RN was the senior pilot and there were also Lieutenant Richards RN and Lieutenant 'Widger' Arnold RN. The party also included two New Zealanders in Woody Woodroffe and Frank Shearman, both of whom added levity to the proceedings. Henry Templeton was to be my observer. A poker school soon formed.

As I had not flown a monoplane before, I had to do a mini-conversion course at Lee before being let loose on the Avenger. And the plane picked for the course was none other than the Hurricane – about as different from the Albacore as the Jaguar is from the horse and cart. I was filled with awe and apprehension. But there wasn't much time to dwell on the possibilities before I was told to get ready and report to the RAF pilot at the hangar apron and he would check me out.

Well, checking out consisted of sitting in the cockpit ready to go but inwardly feeling like my first solo all over again. The unsuspecting Flight Lieutenant leant over the cockpit and merely said:

'There's the starter button, throttle, through the gate for boost, variable pitch control and undercarriage control; no problems? OK; away you go.'

'Lord,' I thought, 'is that all I'm going to know about this powerful thing which I'm supposed to fly?'

But there was not time to sit and think. The groundcrew were ready for me to press the starter tit, the thing roared into action, chocks were away and so was I, careering down the taxi track. The immediate difficulty was the huge engine which made the pilot blind on the ground to anything immediately in front of him. That meant jinxing down the taxi track. However, I got to the off at the end of the runway safely which gave me a feeling for the rudder and throttle. Nothing coming in, nothing taking off so, here goes into wind. Fine pitch, flaps down for take off. A slow push forward on the throttle – boy, that felt like a kick in the back by a mule. What power. Far too exaggerated correction of the rudder in case she swung across the runway which of course she didn't. God, tail up already. Let's go through the gate. Another bloody great punch in the back and my God, we're off the ground. Wheels up (I hope they come down again) coarser pitch, trim OK – what a lovely plane, what an engine.

I was up to 180 mph in no time and beginning to enjoy it. The quick reaction of throttle and controls was a joy. I flew around getting the hang of this magnificent flying machine. It was a new world – this was flying. Why hadn't I opted to be a fighter pilot instead of flying staid old bombers? This was sheer joy. It had to come to an end though and the landing faced. Came in far too fast but there were no problems. She landed like a bird and stayed down. Nor was there any violent swing in the runway. I enjoyed the next two flights even more as I could throw it about a bit but that was the brief encounter I had with the Hurricane before leaving for the Clyde to embark for the United States.

We were to sail in the *Queen Elizabeth*. It was to be a very different voyage than the luxury cruise in *Georgic* to Egypt. The *Queen Elizabeth* was fitted out as a troopship and being an east to west journey the ship was three-quarters empty and was dry. The ship did, however, publish a news sheet called *Elizabethan News* costing 1d. The issue for Sunday, 24th January 1943 reported the fall of Tripoli to the Eighth Army and a heavy RAF raid on Cologne.

As Fleet Air Arm personnel, we did have one diversion. Owing to its speed of 28 knots, the QE sailed alone and unescorted. We were supposed to have better eyesight as flyers and were detailed to keep up a continuous anti-submarine watch from the wings of the Bridge, not the warmest of places in January in mid-Atlantic. In fact we had one piece of excitement when we hit what the captain called the biggest storm he himself had ever experienced in all his years on the Atlantic run. It was at its highest during one of my watches. During the watch, we stood in the little open deck house at far sides of the bridge. Owing to the cut-away of the bows of the ship, it seemed there was nothing between us and the sea far below and I had the most spectacular view of this storm. The snow was being driven by near hurricane force winds. The waves were enormous like vast Mount Everests coming towards us every half minute, each with the spray blown off the top by the tearing wind. The noise was frightening.

The captain had to reduce speed to 15 knots and headed into the wind. 80,000 tons of steel would slide down the back end of a wave with the next one towering above it. As it came to the trough and met the oncoming wave the ship would seem to be halted in its tracks, would just sit there and shudder from stem to stern as if it had been pole-axed. You looked up at the towering angry and wind-torn, grey mass of water in front and wondered how on earth the ship would make it. Every leading edge of the ship was covered thick with frozen snow and it resembled a cork being tossed about by the elements. If ever there was a demonstration of the power of water and wind, that was it. However, make the top of the next wave we somehow did, only to sit momentarily on the wind blown, breaking crest. I wondered whether there was any danger of the ship cracking in half. The gods were certainly angry about something that day.

We were glad to make New York. We anchored outside overnight and next morning sailed into our berth. We were at breakfast when someone shouted to come up on deck. New York at dawn in winter from the Hudson River was one of the most spectacular sights of its kind that I have ever seen. There was a low mist over the city, snow on the ground and a leaden wintry sky. The skyscrapers were pushing their tops above the mist and the lights were twinkling through the gloom. I saw Manhattan many times from a distance but this sight of the city was superb in its winter grey, cold and stark clothing. So this was New York, I thought as I looked out to this wintry dawn, slightly awestruck at seeing America for the first time.

The dockers and tug crews were on strike and the ship had to make its berth on its own. A perfectly timed 90° turn to starboard between two wharves with just enough speed to give the ship the minimum of way. The bows missed the left hand wharf by inches and the starboard beam missed the right hand wharf by a similar amount. Not a scratch, not a bump as the massive ship edged its way perfectly alongside its berth. It was clearly a matter of pride that the captain was determined to make the berth without help, first time and without pranging the boat. It was a really lovely bit of delicate seamanship.

Clearance dealt with, we, the naval passengers, were bussed off to the Barbizon Plaza Hotel on 57th Street West at Central Park South. This was the transit hotel for all naval officers passing through New York and there was an officer in charge of the comings and goings who acted as adviser and counsellor on travel arrangements and anything to do with New York. I couldn't help thinking that that was the job for me. Two of us had a room on the 36th floor from which we looked down Manhattan and over the docks to the right. And what luxury after drab, dark and war-weary Britain and the everlasting sand of the desert! The notice in the room invited the occupant to use the valet service, the laundry, the theatre and concert ticket agency and food and drink in every conceivable form.

'Just phone Room Service.' Suits cleaned and pressed in two hours at 65 cents. Laundry same day at $2 and shoes repaired in a day for $2.65. After using Room Service to the full for the hell of it, getting suits pressed, shoes cleaned and laundry dealt with, we then tucked into triple-decker toasted sandwiches, hamburgers and plenty of local beer. We were all set up to see the town.

On advice from the clerk five of us made our way to the Latin Quarter on Broadway at Times Square. It turned out to be a very good restaurant with a superb floor show lasting over an hour. If you wanted to, you could just sit at a table all evening for the price of the cover charge of $1 an hour and have the minimum of food and drink for not much extra. We took a good view of New York. This city was really something. In sheer size and ostentation it made London in peacetime seem like a series of small towns. The elegance of Fifth Avenue and the lights of Broadway and the vast illumination signs everywhere were staggering especially after the drab dark and dismal war-time London. But it didn't last long. The Admiralty clearly was not going to pay for long for a life of leisure in the big city for young FAA officers and we were soon on our way.

Our destination was Quonset Point, a fairly new and vast naval air station outside Providence, Rhode Island. We travelled there by train and were immediately impressed by its overall size and general air of efficiency and bustle. We were shown to the officers' quarters in a big single-storey block with Coca-cola and ice water machines in the passages. The rooms and cabins were large and comfortable and well furnished. Next door was the mess. The whole was called in American terms the Bachelor Officers' Quarters or BOQ. The mess consisted only of a canteen-like eating area. The food was excellent and served by black stewards in immaculate white suits. Breakfast was milk and orange juice in unlimited quantities and eggs in every shape and form. Invariably the black steward would ask for confirmation: 'Is you aw wantin' yur eggs serney side up.' The mess, like all American naval establishments and ships was dry but just outside the station was an officers' club where food was available and the bar open all hours.

But this was January. The country was flat and the eastern sea board was only a few miles away. The wind blew incessantly and bitingly from the Atlantic, there was snow on the ground and the temperature was always well below zero. The building had fierce central heating and everyone threw off jackets and ties and still sweated. The contrast on sallying forth was enough to take your breath away. Hacking coughs and chest troubles were common and that freezing first month at Quonset was no fun.

But the efficiency of the US navy which I was to meet on many occasions over the next two and a half years was outstanding. There was discipline of course but this was harnessed to the desire to get things done in the quickest and most efficient way. There always seemed to be a wish to get things done without undue respect for rank and form. They were not overburdened by tradition and long usage. You never heard, 'Oh but it has always been done this way.' The way of life was refreshing and invigorating and in this respect the US Navy were only reflecting the mood of the whole country. And the mood was catching. It was not always easy to get along with and one soon learnt the well-worn phrase that America and Britain are two totally different countries, a fact that the common language tends to hide.

One small indication of this difference soon showed up. In their crewroom, in the officers' mess or even when out walking in twos or threes, the American pilots would talk flying and flying tactics ad nauseam, illustrating their point with the two open hands following each other like fighters following another down to the kill. 'Gee, there was I ...' In a British crewroom and certainly in the mess, talk of flying was frowned upon and recounting of personal experiences was taboo. No wonder there was often friction when the two sides met. The American naval pilot looked upon us as puffed-up snobs with an accent that sounded like nothing on earth. Our reticence was

interpreted as a lack of interest. We were an old-fashioned bunch of
fellows from an out-of-date way of life. He had heard little and cared
even less for the struggle for freedom being waged in Europe. The
Battle of Britain and Alamein were unknown to him. His war started
at Pearl Harbour, his enemy was the Jap and he took pride in
Guadalcanal, the hard battles of the Coral Sea and Midway. To us,
he was a brash, cocky, conceited line-shooter confident in his own
destiny, someone who had not yet won his spurs. But as time went
on and particularly as operations against the common enemy
became integrated, a mutual respect grew in spite of different
outlooks and a different way of expressing emotions.

Our offices down on the edge of the airfield were ready for us.
They were smart, functional but reasonably comfortable and well-
equipped. And there were our Avengers lined up on the tarmac.
Their Lordships in their wisdom, renamed the aircraft 'Tarpon' as
all FAA aircraft were traditionally named after birds or fish. Nor had
many people heard of the Tarpon which in fact is a large game-fish
common on the south coast of the US. This crazy-sounding name
for a carrier-borne strike aircraft lasted for a year when sense
prevailed and we reverted to flying the Avenger.

The aircraft had lovely clean lines. It was rather tubby due to the
housing required for the bomb-bay but it looked aerodynamically
sound. It had a Wright Cyclone radial engine which was reliable and
easy to maintain. The view from both cockpits was superb which
made look-out and more importantly deck landings easier. Behind
the rear cockpit was a gun turret with 0.50 calibre gun; one 0.30
calibre gun was in the front position and two 0.50 calibre guns in
the wings. Its maximum speed was 230 knots; it cruised at 160/170
knots; climbed at 130/140 knots and would get up to 330 knots in
a long dive. The wings were said to come off at 350 knots! It had
a reliable undercarriage and for parking on carriers, the wings folded
back and turned to tuck into the fuselage like a bird's wings.

I did not, however, fancy this Avenger when I first climbed in and
started up. The engine clanked like a Tin Lizzy, the plane shook and
the finishing of the airframe was, I thought, poor. But first
impressions turned out to be wrong. I soon began to like it and by
the time I was in carriers, I was thoroughly impressed with its all-
round performance. The Avenger was robust, quick in manoeuvre,

fast in engine reaction, excellent for landing specially on carriers and a good performer for daylight operations. It was a good and very steady dive-bomber.

A word is necessary here on the subject of dive-bombing. This is strictly a misnomer as far as both the Albacore and the Avenger were concerned. The true dive-bomber of World War II was undoubtedly the Ju87 'Stuka' which was purpose built and dived at up to 75°. The Albacore and Avenger were not specialist dive-bombers and would not do more than 45-50°. This was more of a powered glide bomb approach and although the nose was pointed at the target during the dive, it had to be lifted above the target immediately before releasing the bomb. It was perhaps more difficult than strict dive-bombing and needed a lot of judgement and practice to perfect the technique. To all intents and purposes, this was dive-bombing, and with practice, it was very effective. The dive was started between 10,000 and 13,000 feet. It was always best to set a course to the side of the target rather than head-on. In that way, it was easier to adjust the approach and judge the moment to start the dive by dropping one wing, kicking over and getting set in the dive with the target just above the nose. From then on it was hell for leather straight on down to 2,000 – 2,500 feet, making the getaway, as low as possible.

To make up the squadron's aircrew to full strength, we were joined at Quonset Point by newly trained pilots from American flying training schools in Florida. Two who were to become good friends of mine were Gus Halliday (now Vice Admiral Sir Roy Halliday) and Ken Burrenston who was to be brutally murdered by the Japs at the end of the war.

We were to be stationed at Quonset Point from the end of January to the end of May 1943 during which our conversion to Avengers was to be very intense indeed. Wilf Crawford saw to it that we were kept hard at it. Weather permitting, we flew every day, often twice a day and sometimes three times. We were to practise over and over again, navigation, formation flying, dummy torpedo attacks, dive bombing; in fact every aspect of a strike aircraft repertoire. Soon we were to do a good deal of night flying. One aspect of night flying at Quonset that I found disconcerting was the mass of lights on land and particularly in urban areas such as Providence and Newport.

845 Squadron at Quonset Point, Rhode Island, USA.

It made formation flying particularly difficult as the lights of adjacent aircraft got lost in the bright land lights. So different from the desert night flying with the complete blackout but it was never so pitch black that a nearby aircraft could not be seen. Our general area of operations at Quonset was in fact over the sea in a triangle formed by Westerley on the coast, Martha's Vineyard and Block Island to the south near the northern tip of Long Island. However, switching eye from bright lights on and after take off to the pitch black sky over the sea, and vice versa on return was certainly confusing. Dummy deck landings called ADDL's or Assisted Dummy Deck Landings were practised at the small airfield at Westerley or Hyannis on Cape Cod. The routine was relieved by an early trip to Roosevelt Field on Long Island to collect a new aircraft and another to Norfolk, Virginia via Roosevelt Field, Anacostia, Washington and back.

Weekends were usually free days and we could go and do what we liked. Providence was a favourite outing where the Providence Biltmore Hotel was a usual meeting place, but New York called most of all. I was lucky with my leave. When I came back from Egypt, I brought messages for one of the Dekheila officers for his father who ran a timber company in the Aldwych in London. He asked me to a party he was giving at the Savoy; by chance I sat next to a Sid Blair who was an executive in one of the oil companies. By then, I had received my posting to the States and on hearing this, he insisted that I got in touch on arrival in New York with his wife's family who lived in Rye outside New York City and that they would take good care of me. I spent many a weekend with them or their friends, George and Ann Freyermuth who lived nearby at Scarsdale. Nettie Blair made sure that I met as many Americans as possible. The welcome that I got and the hospitality was unbelievable and was such that it can only be found in America. Tickets for this and that and trips round New York were showered on me, the best one being a ticket to Maddison Square Gardens on the night that Beau Jack the middle weight wizard was fighting.

Once, two or three of us were attracted to a restaurant with dancing on Broadway by the sign outside advertising the dancing to Duke Ellington's band. We couldn't resist the sound of good jazz especially by him. A negro band was playing superb jazz and a few were dancing but the barman told us that this was only the Duke's No 2 band. He would be in later. Presently he and his No 1 musicians took over. All dancing and drinking stopped and the customers just crowded round the stage to listen to the wonderful music. He played for an hour non stop. What a feast it was.

Nettie's son Robin was at Choate School. I was pressed into giving a talk to the whole school in their vast theatre about war in the desert. Fortunately, like most Americans at this time, they knew little about the war on the other side of the Atlantic, so I felt I had free rein. But the questions afterwards were pretty searching. On this subject, it surprised me how little the war in Europe and Africa was reported in the American papers. Perhaps there might be a small paragraph tucked away in some papers but you had to search for the news. The American civilian seemed to be much more interested in his own domestic news. Even the Pacific war seemed a long way away from New York.

An American once asked me if it had appeared to me that real life in America was very similar to that portrayed in the movies. I had to admit that it had. He wasn't at all put out but seemed to agree with me.

We were fortunate in sharing Quonset Point with the Air Group of America's latest aircraft carrier, the new *Lexington*. The original *Lexington* had been sunk at the Battle of the Coral Sea in May 1942. Already its successor was built and its aircrews were forming up and training at Quonset prior to leaving for the Pacific. We were very impressed by the size of the new carrier and the power of its Air Group. It gave us an idea of what intense training was really like and the zest and spirit with which the aircrew went about it. I was to see the results later in the war.

By the end of May 1943 we were fully worked up. We had all done about 200 hours flying in the Avenger and by then felt that we were fully in command of the aircraft. One thing was reassuring and that was that it didn't seem to have any vices. Nor did I come across any during the remaining two years of flying the Avenger operationally. So we left Quonset with many regrets and flew to Norfolk, Virginia, or shit-city as it was then known in the American Navy. It was certainly a filthy dirty city but no worse than the average port round the world. Luckily we didn't stay in Norfolk too long.

The day after arrival there we did our first deck landings on USS *Charger*, a small escort carrier and then immediately joined HMS *Chaser* on 1st June. We intensified the deck landing training for a week or two and then left Norfolk with a small convoy bound for New York. It was ironic that I had joined the FAA in 1940 in order to get to sea and it had taken three years to do so.

It may sound strange to say that landing on the deck of a carrier was easier than landing on a runway but in ideal conditions a deck landing certainly had some advantages. In the first place the landing was assisted by a deck landing officer or batsman. He stood on a platform at the after end of the flight deck on the port side. He had a safety net round his platform so that he could throw himself into it if a plane careered towards him. He had two bats like large table tennis bats which he held at arms' length and facing the approaching aircraft. When he held the bats parallel to the ground, it indicated to the pilot that he should continue as he was. Both lowered towards the ground meant, 'Descend quicker', (or you are too high). A frantic lowering of the bats meant: 'For Christ's sake, get down lower and quick'. To get higher (or you are too low) was indicated by the bats being held in a 'V' shape. A frantic action upwards meant, 'Bloody hell, you're going to hit the stern of the ship or worse still, go into the drink.' The batsman crossed the bats below his head to indicate 'Cut engine' or if the approach was hopeless one bat was rotated above the head meaning 'Go round again and make another pass at the deck'. It was essential that the pilot obeyed the batsman's signals instantly and to the letter and if he got the 'Come on as you are' signal, the aircraft would pick up Nos 1, 2 and 3 wires on the deck with his arrester hook which trailed out behind the aircraft's tail.

Secondly, there was no run along the deck which meant no possibility of swinging which could happen on a runway if not checked by use of the rudder.

Finally, the carrier would always be dead into wind for a landing (and take off). Its speed would be adjusted to the speed of the wind so that a plane ideally would be landing into a wind speed of say 30 knots giving the speed of the aircraft over the ground as no more than 45 knots, assuming an airspeed on landing of 75 knots. Apart from the proficiency of the batsman and the pilot, much depended on the feeling of confidence between the two of them.

The aircraft would fly parallel to the ship on the port side on the down wind leg when the undercarriage and arrester hook would be lowered, flaps lowered and propeller set at fine pitch. To avoid a long run in which made the landing more difficult, the turn across wind would be made when the aircraft was on the ship's beam and then the final turn just aft of the ship could be made.

A squadron landing was very much a matter of judgement. The next aircraft should be in the landing approach and about to touch down as the aircraft before it crossed over the lowered barrier on the deck by the island of the carrier so that the barrier would be raised to catch the second aircraft if it missed all the wires.

On landing, the throttle was cut, the wind rolled the aircraft backwards to enable two deck hands to rush out from the sides of the flight deck to release the hook. On the signal being given the pilot raised the hook and opened up the engine to get the aircraft over the barrier as quickly as possible. There was great competition among carrier squadrons to land all twelve aircraft quicker and more efficiently than any other squadron.

The reason for speed was to prevent the carrier or the fleet from steaming on a steady course into wind for longer than absolutely necessary since during the period of landing, the carrier and the accompanying fleet would be vulnerable to submarine or air attack.

The first deck landing was always accompanied by a fit of nerves. From the air, the carrier looked very small and you wondered how on earth you were ever going to get your plane on to that postage stamp of a deck. Then there was the feeling that all eyes in the ship were upon you and waiting for the prang and then 'Will I get one of those wires or will I float over all of them (usually about seven) and go smack into the barrier' which consisted of three thick strands of wire pulled tight between two iron stanchions on each side of the deck. 'Oh God, the plane will be written off and if I get out of it uninjured, I shall be given my marching orders.' By which time the deck of the carrier is coming towards you at a hell of a rate, the batsman is frantically signalling you to come down, he's given you the cut, you've picked up a wire and you are still in one piece. Praise be to God. You are exhausted and you're sweating like a pig but you've done it.

I saw some appalling prangs on the deck. There were planes that went over the side into the drink or missed the round-down (or stern end of the flight deck) and fell in. There was always a guard destroyer to pick up the pilot if he survived. Once an Avenger caught a wire but raced over the port side to end up nose down near the water, but held there by the arrester wire. The pilot took some getting out but the plane had to be cut away into the sea. Then there were the barrier crashes when the aircraft missed all the wires. The plane was a write-off but the pilot usually got away with it. Once a fighter with long range tank landed on successfully but as it came to a halt the tanks blew up and enveloped the whole plane in a sheet of fire. I've never seen a pilot leave a cockpit so quickly.

Those were the days before the modern angled deck. The barrier was there to stop planes on missing the wires, from careering into aircraft parked on the forward end of the flight deck. However, once a Seafire jumped the barrier and ran into the park with terrible casualties.

One of my jobs later on as senior pilot of the squadron was to station myself on the Bridge of Commander (Flying) when I was not flying, to watch and assess the landings of the younger pilots in the squadron and talk to them afterwards to try to iron out any mistakes they were making.

Having been passed for deck landings, the squadron joined HMS *Chaser*, an American built small escort carrier, for passage to England. We left Norfolk on 20th June with a small convoy bound for New York and three days later left New York for England with part of a convoy, rendezvousing with the rest of the ships off Halifax, Nova Scotia. The complete convoy consisted of nearly ninety ships and the area covered by the convoy was immense. We kept continuous anti-submarine patrols in the air throughout daylight hours. A very boring occupation and hard on the backside especially as no one saw anything and the crossing passed off without any incidents.

On arrival in the Clyde, we disembarked to Machrihanish on the Mull of Kintyre and on to RNAS Hatston in the Orkneys. Then began the most soul-destroying, frustrating and futile period I have ever spent in war or peace. The squadron's fortunes went down to a very low ebb while we were there, before we had fired a shot or

Avengers at Hatston –
Orkneys.

dropped a bomb in anger. In spite of enquiries, protests (strictly kept within King's Regulations) noises, hints and so forth, it seemed that Their Lordships were determined to just let us cabbage month after month; or else the file marked 845 Naval Air Squadron had got into the pending basket at Whitehall and had been covered inexorably by piles of paper so that it would never be seen again. It was a case of bungling and bumbling on a costly scale. The only thing that could be said for it was that it didn't cost lives.

It is not difficult to understand why we reckoned that we were the forgotten squadron of the Navy. After six months intense training in America we arrived in England fully trained and worked up, well integrated and capable of giving a good account of ourselves. In other words, ready for operations in any capacity as a strike squadron. We were sent to Hatston in Orkney thinking that this was a stepping-off point to join the Home Fleet. But no. We were destined to stay in Orkney for another six months going over all this training again day after day until we were over-trained, bored and indifferent. We were just flying for flying's sake. We did practise torpedo attacks till we could do them with our eyes closed. I see from my log book that we must have had nearly every ship of the Home Fleet as the target for these attacks. His Majesty's Ships *Shropshire, Belfast, Duke of York, Ceylon, Renown, Anson, Phoebe, Malaya*, USS *Ranger* four times (to show the American Navy what the Royal Navy could do), *London* and *Spartan*. And that is not to mention all the other exercises in the book from dive-bombing, through windfinding to anti-submarine bombing. Once we had a very special torpedo attack on the whole of the Home Fleet. Their Majesties The King and Queen were visiting Scapa Flow and to show off its abilities, the Fleet put to sea with Their Majesties on board HMS *Duke of York*. 845 were commissioned to put on a good torpedo attack and I think we came up to expectations and impressed all concerned.

After six months at Orkney, as if that wasn't enough, we were posted to Machrihanish for a month's anti-submarine bombing practice. Then to Maydown and Eglinton in Northern Ireland near Londonderry for three weeks for further training. We were at last released when there was a panic in the East as the Japs broke through in Burma. So, leaving our planes behind, we, in company with other squadrons embarked for another voyage, this time to

Dummy torpedo attack on Home Fleet off Orkneys.

Ceylon, taking a month to get there. The month of April 1944 was spent in more training until we were rescued by HMS *Illustrious* in May and at last 845 Squadron were on their way to their first operation 17 months and 300 hours personal flying time after forming at Quonset Point. The only thing that can be said for this was that we knew our Avenger. It had certainly been a long engagement.

But to revert to Hatston. If six months further training was to be the order of the day, I can think of no better place to spend it than the Orkneys in the summer and autumn. When we first arrived there, there was almost 24 hours' daylight; the sun did set at about 1 am only to rise again an hour later. It was disconcerting if a good sleep was required but there was no such thing as night. This could be tiring as there was a tendency not to go to bed. The normal routine was upset. However, by December, the days had shortened. It was dark by four o'clock and there was nothing much to do through the long evenings.

October of 1943 seems to have been one of those months of fluctuating fortunes. The saddest and personally the most earth-shattering happening was the death of my mother. She had been weakening for some time, emotionally affected by all three of her sons being in the services and abroad. She had found it difficult at 63 to come to terms with the harsh separation and little news of them. She was finally overtaken by the burden of it all in October. As a youngster I had not realised the seriousness of her illness and when I received a phone call at Hatston from my obviously overcome father to tell me of my mother's death, I felt that the bottom had dropped out of my life. It was a sad and long journey south to the funeral in the old home town.

No sooner had I returned to Hatston than I contracted jaundice and that meant sick bay for a week and then a long convalescence at a Scottish home nearby slowly getting back my strength. I did a lot of thinking during those progresively longer walks along the Orkney lanes and over the fields.

However, during this time, there was a shake-up in the squadron. Wilf Crawford, the CO, and his senior pilot, Johnny Johnson, left and Widger Arnold became the CO and I took over as senior pilot. The greater responsibility brought me back to earth and the realities of life had to be faced.

So it was back to the squadron for three weeks' further training and light flying duties at Hatston before Christmas and Hogmanay celebrations in real Scottish style grounded the squadron until we were due to move south to Machrihanish on 4th January 1944.

As the CO was sick and unable to fly, I had my first taste of leading the squadron to our new base and I enjoyed the new position up front.

The month at Machrihanish on the tip of the Mull of Kintyre was uneventful. It was a month of intense anti-submarine bombing practice always every day and sometimes three or four times a day and at night too. Then as if the Admiralty didn't know what to do with this squadron, we were shunted off to Maydown and Eglinton in Northern Ireland for further training. This way of life was by now wearing very thin. The squadron was losing its spirit and keenness. What was worse was that it was becoming very hard to keep discipline and flying vigilance alive. There was a feeling that we were surplus to requirements and no one in high authority cared what we did or how we did it. We were fast losing our edge. Nobody told us what we were doing, why we were doing it and what was our future.

The truth began to emerge. For some years, the Admiralty had been working on the development of a strike aircraft to take the place of the Swordfish and Albacore. The original design was heavy and cumbersome. The aircraft manufacturers did what they could with a poor specification but the Admiralty then got hold of the prototype and added this and modified that until the finished article was a real bastard to fly. It looked like a Christmas tree and flew like a pig. They called it the Barracuda. It was lethal. Many an aircrew were killed through failure to come out of a dive or just plain inexplicable failures. It was a real brute but the Admiralty persevered in spite of appalling non-operational losses.

I must have been out of my mind when I volunteered to fly a Barracuda in Ceylon while we were based there later in 1944. I wanted to see for myself just what this disreputable plane was like. I've never had such a hairy flight and was really relieved to get down in one piece. The Merlin engine sounded good on start up. I got to the end of the long runway at Katukurunda in Ceylon and opened up to take-off. I needed full power to get it even moving and I started trundling along the runway. It was sluggish, heavy and cumbersome; there was no feeling of power. Half way along the runway, by which time the Avenger would have left the runway, we were nowhere near becoming unstuck. I began to get worried as the end of the runway and the sea ahead loomed up on me. We took the whole length of the runway and then I had to yank her into the air. We staggered up to 1,000 feet and turned into the circuit. By now, I was determined not to try any fancy things with it but to get back to the airfield as quickly as possible. It was like flying a tank. Any resemblance to an aircraft was coincidental. It had no reaction on the throttle and the answer I got from the controls was like trying to move a dead weight. I gave myself plenty of room on the run in to land and by force of habit with the Avenger I cut the throttle to a minimum short of the runway specially, as I had kept my speed purposely on the high side. The plane started to fall out of the sky and I got the willies. God, I'm not going to make it. I jammed the throttle to full power and the Barracuda only just cleared the end of the runway.

I told Wings – the station's Commander Flying – when I got out, 'Don't ever make me fly that bastard again.'

He just grinned and said, 'You didn't have to, did you?' but I didn't see the joke.

For some patriotic reason, the Admiralty went ahead and equipped a lot of squadrons with the Barracuda including carrier squadrons; while at the same time they were going ahead with the formation of Avenger squadrons in the US including 845 Squadron. We were put into a backwater of incessant training while aircrews were losing their lives flying this pig of an aircraft. Eventually, but too late for many pilots of the Barracuda, sense prevailed and the Avenger replaced the Barracuda on all the carriers and most importantly in the British Pacific Fleet to be formed later that year.

But to return to 845. We received a hurried signal to embark the personnel of the squadron, after a short home leave for all, in the *Strathnaver* on 2nd March. We were able to go through the Mediterranean this time. We arrived at Port Said on 16th March, changing ships to SS *Aronda* and got to Colombo on 5th April.

We were soon at our new base, Royal Naval Air Station at Katukurunda. This was a completely new way of life from that in

England, America and the desert and there were a lot of local variations to get used to. The airfield itself was new and fairly basic. Just one long concrete runway hewn out of the jungle and ending on the shore. Planes were dispersed around about in the jungle and with the ever present backcloth of palm trees. Flying tended to take place in the mornings and late afternoon. It was too hot to be out in the sun after lunch and a zizz was the usual routine. The morning activities started very early in the cool of the day. A quick breakfast of paw-paw and coffee and then to the bus for the two mile journey to the airfield. Elevenses were at 10.30 but not with coffee. Native boys had been spending the morning shinning up trees to collect coconuts, pineapples, bananas, paw-paws and would come round dispersals with the exotic fruit in baskets. Each piece of fruit was the equivalent of one penny. The huts which contained the bedrooms or cabins, and the mess itself, were all thatched with open sides. Every building had a pathway round it covered by the thatch roof to prevent the rain driving into the rooms. All buildings were single-storey.

The weather was strange too. On arrival in Ceylon at the beginning of April, we were told that the monsoon would begin on a certain day in the first week in May. And it did. Before the monsoon, the weather was hot, sunny and humid; typically tropical. And suddenly on the day predicted, the heavens opened, the clouds were low and black and the rain came down relentlessly and monotonously in sheets like I've never seen rain before. This was the south-west monsoon. Paths and tracks became rivers and humidity rose to 100°. You sat and dripped with sweat pouring down your body, making every part of you stick to chairs while the rain poured and poured outside. This was one of the more uncomfortable of the earth's climates. After a week or so of these conditions, gaps in the rain would turn up and get longer and longer and after a month or so, the weather would turn showery and then fine.

So it would remain until the north-east monsoon began in October. This one however, was not nearly so intense. It would be more showery with light rain and the monsoon would be over well before Christmas. The humidity, however, was devastating. Cigarettes and matches became damp overnight and had to be dried out in the sun before a smoke could be enjoyed. Clothes hanging in a wardrobe soon became mouldy and would be ruined if left there. The native boys who looked after us and the cleaning of the cabins didn't understand the dangers of humidity. It was important to hang suits out in the open air every other day. One of the fellows didn't do this and lost all his suits and clothes to the dreaded mildew at a great cost of replacement.

We had the constant companionship of families of monkeys in the palm trees nearby and on the cabin roof. Sometimes their frolicking and raucous noise were a bit too much, and it tended to wake the whole neighbourhood at the crack of dawn. And we were welcomed to 'Kat' on our first day by the sight of a huge python that had been caught and overcome near the camp and was then strung up on a line. It had squeezed and eaten a lamb and a native. It looked monstrous and dangerous even in death and plenty of us were tempted to ask for a transfer back to the UK. There were plenty of snakes of all types, large and small and it was as well to shake out shoes in the morning lest one had gone in overnight for a snug sleep. The heat and humidity remained through the night so that little sleep under the mosquito nets was possible.

One great treat, however, was Sunday lunch in the mess. It was a help yourself, have as much as you like affair. Six large dishes and about twenty small ones with bits and pieces. It was curry as it should be made. After two heaped plates of that, the only thing to do was to get into the Jeep, go down to the beach and select the shade of a nice palm tree for a zizz, and then a bathe.

Strangely enough, the bar was not well stocked. Beer was rationed to two small bottles a week each and there were no spirits apart from an occasional input of Indian gin flown down by a pilot who might be calling in at Madras. What was left was a plentiful supply of all types of liqueurs. One evening we had a school of twelve all drinking a different liqueur. Someone spotted this and suggested it would be easier to order twelve of every type, mix them in a jug and share it out. The result was a filthy-looking muddy-coloured drink with an even filthier taste. What sacrilege and what hangovers next day!

We had our better days, however, at Lavinia Beach and in Colombo which had plenty to offer in the form of entertainment.

If the coast was hot heavy and humid, the hills were fresh, cool and sunny and it was a joy to go up there for leaves. I went twice to Nuwara Eliya and once to a tea plantation at Silver Kandy. They were both some 5,000 feet up and Nuwara Eliya could be anywhere in the highlands of Scotland. It also had a lovely and challenging golf course. On about every hole a stream meanders across the fairway at about 200 yards. Two caddies were therefore essential, one to carry your bags and the other stationed on the bank of the stream to spot your ball as it falls into the water and then to wade in and retrieve the ball with a small net on the end of a long bamboo pole. Invariably one's drive goes in the stream. While your caddie is telling you that the fore-caddie will get it out with his net, the said fore-caddie is picking the ball up between his toes and hiding it in his pyjama-like suit. When you get there, you are met with, 'Master, can't find ball, water too muddy, ball lost.' It and many like it then go on sale outside the clubhouse. I swear I was offered one of mine back to me with the comment, 'No, Master, ball found in rough.' It is all part of the fun.

Another hazard of that testing golf course came to light on my first round. Nuwara Eliya has an above average rain fall and the surrounding mountains are often covered in cloud and mist. The course is therefore on the damp side specially the rough which consists of long wet grass. It wasn't long before I was in the rough hacking about to find my ball. Soon the lower part of my leg started itching. I pulled up my trousers to find big black slugs – leeches – having a good tuck in at my blood. The sight of them first time nearly made me sick. I soon learnt that it was useless to flick or pull them off as they left their snout in your flesh and it went on sucking. The most effective remedy was to put a lighted cigarette to their tail and they would then fall away, snout and all. As I was a fairly heavy smoker there was no problem in having the remedy handy. Though one got used to the dreadful little beasts, a drive into the rough invariably meant the loss of ball and blood.

I came across two examples of the old Colonial days. I'm glad I did meet them before those days passed away for good. The first was during a week's stay at the tea plantation at Silver Kandy not far from Nuwara Eliya. The planter who was an Englishman of the old school lived there on his own. He had a lovely bungalow high up in the hills with lovely views over the uplands towards the coastal strip and the sea. The nights were cool and the days hot and dry.

(Left) Dhobie time in Ceylon. *(Right)* Ceylon.

Mount Lavinia – Ceylon 1944.

The bungalow was run by the servant boys and Master was good to them. Breakfast was when you felt like it and the choice of food was immense; the head boy (aged about 50) brought you your every request.

Then after a suitable interval to digest the meal, planter and I went out in the fields where the tea leaves were being picked from the low bushes by a gang of Singalese women. There we met the manager and foreman for a discussion on the day's work, the quality of the crop, collection of the leaves and future planting followed by a personal inspection of the crop. Back to the bungalow for a frugal lunch followed by an afternoon kip. Tea on the verandah, Edwardian style, and then at six sharp; 'I say, old man, have a peg,' a clap of hands and at that moment the head boy would enter.

'Two pegs, Charlie.' A wonderful atmosphere of the sun going down and a whisky by your side. Little is said. There may be a war on to decide whether Communism, Fascism or Democracy will rule the world but just here in the hills of Ceylon, on a balcony overlooking a tea plantation, God is in his heaven and all is well with the world.

A quick but formal dinner after the ration of two pegs each and then, 'I say, old man, would you like to go along to the Planters Club?' The Victoria Club nearby was fairly full of other local planters and their wives. The conversation that was about as fatuous as can be imagined was mostly concerned with local intrigues and gossip and looked no further than the arrival of the mail boat from the UK. It wasn't my sort of scene with its emptiness and pretension but I'm glad to have seen this type of Colonial life which was shortly to end. I enjoyed the comfort of it all, though I was glad to get back to the realities of life.

The other example of local life was quite different but was still part of a life long since gone by. There was a rubber plantation not far from Kat situated in the hot and humid jungle. It was managed by a very gregarious Scot from Dundee who enjoyed entertaining Service personnel at his bungalow. There were never less than twenty and often many more airmen, sailors and Wrens who all enjoyed his Scottish evenings. They were full of fun and life with Scotch and Eightsome reels and bagpipes and haggis. Tiny, on account of his vast size, couldn't get away from all that Scotland meant to him and so recreated the atmosphere in the unlikely spot of his jungle bungalow. He was a great man in every way who loved giving fun to as many people as he could.

CHAPTER NINE

Action at last

Soon after arriving in Ceylon and shaking down at Katukurunda, we heard the great news that we were to join HMS *Illustrious* albeit on a temporary basis for one big operation. We were to replace the carrier's Barracuda squadron because, apart from the many superior features of the Avenger, it could carry a heavier load of bombs for a greater distance. The idea of including us brought excitement to us all after the long dreary months of training with no operational plan to aim for. And what better ship than *Illustrious* for our debut. This wasn't an ordinary aircraft carrier, it had a name and a reputation above all others.

After a practice deck landing or two on HMS *Unicorn*, eight of us landed on *Illustrious*, with 832 Squadron making up the Avenger contingent, the fighter squadron being Norman Hanson's experienced and resident 1833 Corsair Squadron. We were to carry out the operation with the air group of the USS *Saratoga*, a very experienced carrier that had been lent by the Americans to the Eastern Fleet and had already carried out operations with the British in the Indian Ocean.

As soon as we had landed on, the Captain of *Illustrious*, Captain Cunliffe, invited the senior officers of the squadron to his cabin to meet him and have a drink with him. As in all such British Service gatherings, the atmosphere was quiet, formal and stilted. But presently the door swung open and in came an American Commander, a large man in every sense. He went straight up to the Captain, slapped him on the back and bawled, 'Gee, hiya, Captain, how's the hangover?' This was Commander 'Jumping Jo' Clifton, the famous and very experienced Air Group Commander from the *Saratoga*.

From that moment on, formality vanished, rank was forgotten and the party started. Jumping Jo filled the room with his presence

RNAS Katukurunda.

845 Squadron at RNAS Katukurunda.

and his booming voice and made us Avenger pilots completely at home. He had the American capacity to enjoy life, to get the most out of it, and whatever he did, was done with wholehearted commitment. His zest was infectious and he couldn't fail to inspire anyone who came into contact with him. A robust sense of humour and a thoroughly earthly outlook rounded off a larger than life character. He seemed glad to have three more squadrons equipped with American aircraft under his leadership and was clearly delighted to have the *Illustrious* Air Group under his command.

We left Colombo on 6th May with *Saratoga* and the cruisers *Ceylon* and *Gambia* meeting up outside with the rest of the fleet, the *Queen Elizabeth, Valiant, Renown*, the French battleship *Richelieu* and the Dutch cruiser *Tromp* together with destroyers. We began a long journey south. Soon after leaving, we were told that our target was to be Japanese installations at Surabaya on the north coast of Java. But as the trip there and back was too far for the fuel carried by the fleet, we would first call in at Exmouth Gulf on the north-west coast of Australia to refuel. The plan was for the dive-bombing Dauntlesses from *Saratoga* to destroy the oil refinery at Wonokromo near Surabaya, then the American Avengers would attack the port and any shipping in it, while *Illustrious*'s Avengers would bomb the Braat Engineering works nearby. Braat was the largest works of its kind in the Dutch East Indies.

We did two big practice strikes on the way down, dive-bombing exercises on *Renown* and on *Illustrious*. Exmouth Gulf was a huge natural harbour but the only signs of life were our refuelling tankers. Otherwise, it was a dreary spot with nothing to commend it. So after refuelling we steamed north again but this time to the south coast of Java.

The operation took place on 17th May. Our bomb load was four 500 lb bombs. We had to fly some 80 miles to the coast and then over the mountains and volcanoes to fly over Java for 100 miles to the north coast. We had our final briefing from Commander (operations) and Squadron Commanders. In the middle of this, the door flew open and in came Jumping Jo Clifton. There was no doubting his presence as he jumped up on the platform and addressed us in a loud booming and aggressive voice. His message was short and direct:

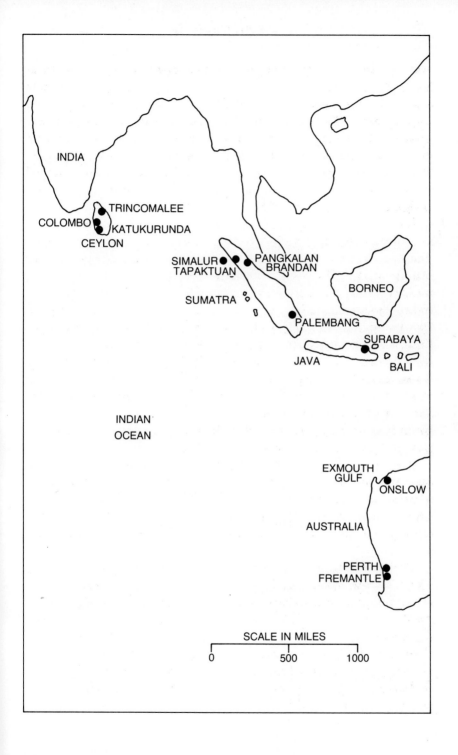

INDIA

TRINCOMALEE
COLOMBO
KATUKURUNDA
CEYLON

SIMALUR
TAPAKTUAN
PANGKALAN
BRANDAN

SUMATRA

PALEMBANG

BORNEO

SURABAYA
JAVA
BALI

INDIAN
OCEAN

EXMOUTH
GULF
ONSLOW

AUSTRALIA

PERTH
FREMANTLE

SCALE IN MILES
0   500   1000

'OK, boys, if I tell you go dig a hole, you'll go right out and dig the biggest hole you ever dug. If I tell you to get out there and hit those yellow bastards, you will tear into them and knock the living daylights out of them. That's all – best of luck – keep hitting 'em and hard.'

And he was gone. We were to hear him next day over the air leading the boys from the front and calling for attack and aggression and launching into anyone who appeared to be trailing or in his view not trying. It was rather like a boxer's second shouting at his charge to get stuck in and murder his opponent.

This was the first time that I had seen the American Navy flyers at work on a carrier and against the enemy. We had been brought up on the supremacy of the Royal Navy but to see the Americans operating was a revelation and an illusion completely shattered. There was a single-minded aggression about them, from the deck hands, through to the aircrews to the Air Group Commander. Their deck work was proficient to the last detail, the work of the aircrew in the air was as keen and sharp as a razor blade. No doubts entered their minds. The Japs were going to be defeated lock, stock and barrel; the only reservation was how long it would take. The Americans approached the task as if every punch was the KO punch. I was to see it in greater depth and in far greater numbers later in the Pacific. There was a relentlessness and inexorable quality in their naval operations that was to take them from near defeat at Pearl Harbour and later in the South Pacific to total victory in the vast arena of the Pacific; like a boxer down and nearly out in the first round, coming back to win by a KO in the tenth.

This was to be a full range of aircraft on deck ready for the take-off. And here was another indication of the greater power of the Americans. *Saratoga* ranged up on deck over fifty aircraft consisting of Hellcat fighters, Dauntless dive-bombers and strike Avengers. *Illustrious*'s ranged just sixteen Corsair fighters and sixteen Avengers. So, by sheer numbers, it was predominantly an American operation. We learnt a lot from their methods.

The aircraft were ranged overnight with wings folded. Fighters in front as they needed a shorter run than the bombed up Avengers. Shaken at 0500. Dressed in flying overalls and soft shoes, making sure not to carry any private papers. Butterflies in the tummy and half asleep but with a fearful realisation that this was it. God, can't they cancel it? I wish I wasn't here. To the wardroom for a good breakfast of bacon and eggs, toast and coffee. Don't feel like it. Feel more like a condemned man being given the obligatory breakfast before facing the noose. No talking except for one or two who had to vent their nerves with cheap jokes – wish they would shut up.

Action stations blaring throughout the ship. Noise and pandemonium let loose. Collect Mae West and helmet and make way to the ready room in the island. Someone says it's a fine morning. Wish it would rain. The silence of aircrews sitting emotionally and with their own thoughts is broken by the order 'Man your aircraft.'

We jump to it and race across the dawn-lit and windy flight deck to our aircraft. Up on the wings and into the cockpit. The fear is still there but it begins to take a back seat as there are now many things to do. Two groundcrew follow up the wings and help with fixing parachute harness and safety strap. Check around the cockpit, look around at the parked aircraft. Hope the engine starts, will look a proper Charlie if it doesn't as that will hold up the take-off. There is a strange hush on deck as the fleet turns quickly into wind.

No sooner straight and Commander (Flying) from the bridge calls through the loudspeaker, 'Corsairs start up.' The silence is broken into a deafening din of sixteen engines. Then 'Avengers start up,' and the din is appalling.

The deck officer takes over and waves the fighters, first to the centre of the deck, wings are extended and then the first one roars along the flight deck, followed in quick succession by everyone else. God, what the hell am I doing here, is everything OK, fine pitch, wings locked – it's me now. Oh! My God, it's me. Scared stiff and shaking as I open the throttle to full but keep the brakes on. At full revs, take the toes off the brakes and start rolling. The wind over the deck makes it feel as if the aircraft is hardly moving. Pass the island and the end of the flight deck looks ominously near. I won't make it. But it's too late. I can't stop now. The heavily laden Avenger falls off the end of the deck and sinks to sea level. But she is flying. Will I clear the sea?

Up wheels quickly and a jinx to starboard to clear the slipstream and gradually but ever so gradually the plane becomes stable and starts climbing. The only obviously good thing is the feeling that you're on your own away from the panic and hubbub reigning on deck. That is a relief. But now to chase the others in front to 2,000 feet for the big form up. I only have to worry about Widger Arnold the leading Avenger as I have to get tucked in behind and below his flight of four, with my flight chasing to join up with me. Both flights are to fly diamond formation. There are the Americans doing the same. We turn to port and again to make for the forming up area astern and then look for the Americans to form up on them.

Well, that was a good form-up. The engine is going well. All the dials are registering normal, oil temp and pressure OK. Can relax a bit and look around. It is a lovely sunny day and there is Java ahead like a dark misty blue wall. Soon we start climbing at 130 knots. I don't like this. More throttle required and it is not easy to keep station. We are up to 12,000 feet and level off. Hell, we are crossing the coast and looking straight into the jaws of a volcano. There are quite a lot of them along the coast, some smoking idly. Hope they don't erupt. And there is Java laid out before us. What a lovely looking country. Wouldn't mind living here – but not just yet, please God.

And there is the sea on the other side. Surabaya slightly to our left and there to the right is Bali. During briefing, we were told if anything happened to us we should make for Bali. 'They are friendly people.' Just at that moment I had the urge to break away and spend the rest of the war in Bali. What a thought. But come on, keep your eye on the ball it may be for real if you don't look out. We are there, the Braat works are easy to spot. We deploy and keel over for the dive. It is a long way down but we're soon at 3,000 feet; press the tit at 2,500 feet with the works looming large just above the engine cowling. Bombs away and pull out quickly feeling the pull in the stomach. Make for the rendezvous. Bill Thomson, my observer, tells me the bombs scored a bull's eye; turn and look at the morning's work; the works are a shambles and smoking.

Now, for the reforming, no problem in that and we are all there. We had taken them completely by surprise and there was no opposition. Poor chaps were caught at breakfast. Up to 8,000 feet again and heading back home to the safety of *Illustrious*. Over the volcanoes again and let down on the other side. There is the fleet.

Take-off from *Illustrious.*

On the way to attack Sourabaya, Java.

We are nearly there. Break off from the Americans and make for the carrier. It seems to sit low in the water compared to *Saratoga*. We peel off ahead of the ship and make a good and quick squadron landing. Make for the forward lift, fold wings and at the signal from the deck officer, cut engine. Get out and make for ops room for debriefing.

It has been a highly successful operation. All our bombs hit the target and all of *Illustrious*'s chicks returned safely. We felt proud and elated, if a bit drained. I don't think we let the veteran carrier down. Now for the beer.

The next day *Saratoga* and her destroyers left us to return to the Pacific. It was an emotional farewell as she sailed down our port side, the flight deck of both carriers being lined with aircrews and ships' companies cheering and waving their goodbyes. She was a great ship with a brave and very efficient Air Group led superbly by Commander 'Jumping Jo' Clifton USN.

The attack on Surabaya was reported in the London *Evening News* on 24th May under the headline 'London Men Hit Surabaya. They watch Jap Admiral Run' as follows:

> London airmen, it is revealed to-day, took part in the war's first big attack on Surabaya, the great Jap naval base in the Dutch East Indies, on May 17.
>
> It was believed that a powerful Jap Fleet in the Singapore area included battleships and heavy cruisers, while several Jap submarines were seen in Surabaya naval harbour during the attack.
>
> Yet the Allied warships were unmolested from the air or sea.
>
> It was a half-hour blitz. Planes and carriers went in and came out again without a scratch.
>
> ### The Admiral Ran
>
> In a breakfast-time swoop British and US pilots destroyed an oil refinery, two engineering works, hit ships in the harbour and wrecked at least 20 planes.
>
> About 100 planes attacked the base. Diving down so low that they could plainly make out the gold lace on a fleeing Jap Admiral's chest, British pilots smashed the naval workshops

(*Right*) Attack on Sourabaya, Java.

(*Below*) USS *Saratoga* saying farewell to HMS *Illustrious*.

and completely destroyed the Braat Engineering Works.

Pilots who smashed the Braat works included Lieutenant Donald Judd, of Guildford, Sub-Lieutenants Charles Williams, of Lewisham, Roy W Halliday, of Kingsbury, and John E Randell, of Alexandra Park.

Sadly, the squadron had to leave *Illustrious* on returning to Trincomalee. I had enjoyed my first taste of life on board a Fleet carrier. After some leave in the hills we were to be down-graded. We were to join HMS *Ameer*, an escort carrier for anti-submarine work. At least we would be afloat but as it turned out, 845 was to continue its boring and frustrating existence. We joined *Ameer* at the end of June and made for the straits between Ceylon and India and then into Trincomalee for three weeks to wait for suitable escorts.

At the beginning of August we set sail for Colombo preparatory to going out on patrol but on arrival the ship's engines broke down and it looked as if the ship would be stuck there indefinitely. That raised a problem. Not only was *Ameer* unserviceable but it had a full squadron of Avengers on board rendered completely impotent. Not only that, but life on board an escort carrier in that heat was unbearable. Escort carriers were very basic with few built in comforts. The cabins and the wardroom were small. With nothing to do but wait and see, we went ashore as much as possible. But a run ashore after six in the evening meant a change into full white uniforms with the jacket fastened to the neck. But it was impossible to look smart as the uniform was wringing wet with perspiration before you were fully dressed. It was no good changing as the same thing would happen. You entered the liberty boat feeling like a wet fish. A fine way to set out to meet the girl friend for dinner at the Galle Face Hotel. Fortunately, every one was in the same condition. Also, the dhobi arrangements were so good that a suit sent for cleaning after breakfast would be back after lunch beautifully laundered and starched.

However, something had to be done about the aircraft and there was plenty of discussion between the Captain, the Engineer Commander and the Senior Pilots. Between monsoons there was little wind in Ceylon. That rules out a normal deck take off in harbour. How about the catapult? But this could be dangerous in

Avenger crashes on landing on HMS *Ameer*.

Seafire jumps the barrier.

Avenger takes off from the catapult.

Avenger approaching to land.

Corsair approaching to land on HMS *Ameer*.

Corsair lands on HMS *Ameer*.

Long range tank explodes (the pilot was saved).

Barrier crash.

no-wind conditions with all the obstructions that exist in harbours. The Engineer promised us as much power as he could muster and it was decided to have a go. The prospect of boredom and heat in a broken-down carrier in Colombo harbour entrance ensured approval of the pilots even at the risk of the first one, who was me, falling into the harbour. Finally all was well and we got the planes off though it was a close run thing. This meant a return to Katukurunda for yet more training but that was the better of two evils.

But salvation was at hand. The Eastern Fleet was being strengthened and during 1944 ships were coming out from the UK for this purpose. The original idea was for the Eastern Fleet to operate in the Indian Ocean in support of the Americans pushing in on Japan across the Pacific but the idea had been forming for some time that an efficient and fast Task Force would be formed out of the Eastern Fleet to join the Americans in the Pacific. Negotiations had been going for some time to this end between a keen Admiralty and a reluctant Washington.

One of the carriers to arrive in Ceylon in July was *Victorious*; it had as its Air Group, 1834 and 1836 Squadrons, flying Corsairs and 849 Squadron with Avengers. The CO of 849 turned out to be my old friend David Foster; we had done our flying training in the same No 13 course. It was good to see him again and we talked of old times and prospects for the future.

When he heard of the situation with 845, he said, 'I badly need an experienced Senior Pilot specially if we are to go round to the Pacific. Now, I know about my higher rank as CO of the squadron but we have the same seniority in the FAA. Would you be prepared to sink your pride and join me as Senior Pilot of 849. I would like it but would you?'

I jumped at the opportunity of joining another Fleet carrier and getting round to the Pacific. We shook hands on it. He also wanted more experienced Avenger pilots too and I suggested I bring with me Gus Halliday and Ken Burrenston. They both liked the idea. So, clearances were obtained from *Victorious* and from Widger Arnold and negotiations were completed with Flag Officer Air, East Indies in Colombo and I finally left 845 and joined 849 at the end of October 1944 at Katukurunda. We did some intensive flying in the

Facing page: (Top) Avenger in flight. *(Bottom)* Avenger taking off from carrier.

(Right) The Senior Pilot (the Author) and Senior Observer (Freddie Willett) 849 Squadron.

(Below) 849 Squadron at Katukurunda.

The Author's Flight in 849 Squadron Katukurunda.

new squadron and in Group exercises with the other carriers, *Illustrious, Indomitable* and *Indefatigable* before landing on *Victorious* outside Trincomalee on 19th December. *Victorious* turned out to be a very happy ship whose captain, Michael Denny, did everything he could to help the aircrews and was very approachable. Charles Owen was Commander Operations.

The Admiral in command of the carriers was none other than Philip Vian of *Cossack* fame. He had been in command of the destroyers on the journey to Egypt in *Georgic* and had been instrumental in sealing the fate of *Bismarck*. He flew his flag in *Indomitable*. I saw quite a lot of him during the next six months, usually before and after an operation. Although not an aviator himself, he set his mind on mastering the techniques of flying on operations from carriers. He always had the welfare of his aircrew at heart. The COs and Senior Pilots of squadrons were encouraged to talk and give their views and criticisms. He always asked searching questions about tactics and having satisfied himself that everyone had had their say, he would make his decisions quickly and positively. He commanded everyone's respect.

One very bizarre episode occurred after joining *Victorious*. It was announced that Noël Coward who was in India entertaining the troops, would be paying a visit to the Fleet at Trincomalee for one concert. The perfect setting was one of the aircraft carriers. The after aircraft lift would be lowered to just above the hangar level to provide the stage. The auditorium would be after part of the hangar cleared of aircraft. The great evening arrived and selected parties of officers and ratings descended on the chosen carrier. The hangar held a large audience and there were others sitting on the rim of the flight deck looking down on the stage. Now there is no more basic audience than that provided by naval ratings. They want dirty songs and dirty jokes, nothing sophisticated, nothing clever, just good old music hall jokes, dirty and corny.

Poor Noël Coward came in with his pianist both dressed in white tuxedoes which was a bad start. After a suitable introduction from the Captain, he launched into his most sophisticated West end night club repertoire in his inimitable voice. It was clearly not to the liking of the British Jack Tar. Soon chairs began to be shifted which made a clatter on the steel hangar deck, then comments in the naval style began to be audible and finally those sitting in the rim of the flight deck started dropping coins on the steel lift below acting as a stage. Noël Coward couldn't take it any longer and went off in a huff followed by embarrassed Captain, Commander and other top brass.

The sailors, who are nothing if not fair-minded, must have realised they had gone too far. After a long interval Coward returned, changed his tune a bit and was heard out in the second half. It was not one of his most successful concerts or his most receptive audience.

CHAPTER TEN

Pangkalan Brandan

Three weeks after joining *Victorious* with 849 Squadron, we left Trincomalee on New Year's day 1945 bound for an attack on an oil refinery in Eastern Sumatra – code named Operation Lentil. The Fleet consisted of three carriers, *Indomitable*, *Victorious* and *Indefatigable* with cruisers *Argonaut*, *Black Prince*, *Ceylon* and *Suffolk* and eight destroyers. These ships made up Force 67. The target was the oil refinery at Pangkalan Brandan near Medan on the Malacca Straits. An attack had been made by aircraft of the Fleet some two weeks before but this was seriously affected by bad weather. On that occasion the Fleet had entered the Malacca Straits before launching its aircraft for the attack. This time it was decided to change the fly-off position to a point between the island of Simalur and Sumatra off the Western or Indian Ocean side of Sumatra. This would mean a difficult flight over the Wilhelmina range of mountains which rose to 10,000 feet before flying over the Sumatran plain to the target on the opposite coast.

In all, the operation was to be carried out by 92 aircraft. The strike itself consisted of sixteen Avengers from *Indomitable*, twelve Fireflies armed with rockets from *Indefatigable* and sixteen Avengers of 849 Squadron from *Victorious*. The Avengers were armed with four 500 lb bombs. Sixteen Corsairs from *Victorious* would act as escort with sixteen Hellcats from *Indomitable*. In addition eight Hellcats from *Indomitable* and eight Corsairs from *Victorious* would form what were called Ramrods, that is, a force of fighters sent off some time before the main strike to soften up the opposition particularly by attacking airfields on the way to and around the target to catch the enemy fighters before they could take off.

We had worked out what we thought was the ideal formation for the Avengers. We were in three flights of 6-6-4. Each flight was stepped down and the individual flight flew in half vics of two planes

849 Squadron on HMS *Victorious*.

each, closely stepped down. In this way, it was thought that maximum manoeuvrability could be achieved while at the same time providing the maximum fire power for the rear turrets against attacking fighters. After form-up which was achieved quickly and successfully, we were to approach the coast as low as possible to get underneath any Jap radar that they might have on that coast, and then climb steeply up over the mountains to 12,000 feet letting down to about 10,000 feet over the plain and the approach to the target. The 2,000 feet let down was designed to make speed on the vulnerable approach.

The ramrods took off soon after 0600 while the main strike took off at 0730. Another shake at 0500, after a night of little sleep, and over two hours of jittery, testy feelings and a fear of that dreadful unknown out there. The unwanted breakfast thrust in front of the aircrew, the long and painful wait in the ready room and then all hell let loose on the order to man aircraft. The wind over the deck, the shouts of the deck officers and their handlers and finally the deafening noise of all the engines starting up together. There go the fighters. David Foster is the first Avenger to go. I am seventh with my flight of six behind me.

Here we go, staighten up on the centre line of the Flight deck, watch the deck officer who is rotating his arm above his head, a signal for me to jam on my brakes and rev up to maximum. He drops his hand in the direction of the bows, off brakes and go. The old girl sounds OK as we trundle up the deck and just make it off the end of the deck. Then a chase after David and his five. He has throttled back and kept straight ahead of the carrier to give the squadron a chance to form up quickly. He does a gentle turn to port which gives us a chance to cut corners. My new observer, George Graham, tells me that he and the air gunner, Petty Officer Murphy, are OK and then keeps me informed about my flight forming up on me. Apart from my No 2 on my starboard quarter I can't see the others as they are behind and below me.

The complete form up is good. The day is bright and clear. All is well. We fly over the sea very low towards those mountains some forty miles away. They look low on the horizon but I know they are 10,000 feet high. They look lovely in the misty blue haze of the morning. We are over the coast and the strike leader starts climbing.

We are very soon climbing up the mountains. Hey, this is a steep climb, I thought. I need nearly full throttle and finer pitch of the airscrew to keep up. Hope my chaps can follow me. We seem to be sandwiched in between David's flight and the mountains. Speed barely 130 knots and high revs so there is not much margin for manoeuvre if that should become necessary. We're hanging on our props. The mountains look forbidding; rocky, rough, steep and covered in trees. We are too close to them for comfort; I'm not enjoying this.

And then it happens ... the engine coughs and splutters. Christ, what's happening; I've no time to check dials as I immediately lose height and speed and drop out of the formation. All I can do is to turn towards the coast about five miles away and get the nose down. The engine sounds bad. It is missing more than ever. I was at 5,000 feet when it happened and it looks as if I shall have to glide down without much help from the engine. Smoke begins to pour out of it and it all but stops. Anyway there is no power there. I tell George what I'm doing and discuss ditching procedures and broadcasting our position. But will I make the coast or will we be calling in on the natives or the Japs for breakfast? Oh! God, save me from that.

I lengthen the glide as much as I dare. Even if I make the sea I shall be broadcasting my presence and either the Japs or the locals will come out to get us. There is a town somewhere here called Tapakyuan. Good, we are over the coastal strip at 1,500 feet; we should make the sea OK.

'Get ready to ditch. Will drop the bombs as soon as we get over the sea.'

If nothing else, they will hear the bombs hit the water – can't be helped. No wind to speak of so I can land along my flight path thus making as much distance as possible betweeen us and the shore. Flaps down, keep wheels up. Here we go: 'Hold on – about to land.' Pull up nose so that the tail hits the water first; then we ski along the water for a short distance, the engine smoking like fun and hissing. Good, we came to a rest the right way up. Murphy is out of the back like lightning and inflating the dinghy, George is getting into it. I waste no time in getting out of the cockpit and down the wing to get into the dinghy when I remember my cap and go back for it. That seems silly but it was lucky that I did, as the sun was

Forming up for attack on Pangkalan Brandan.

Range of aircraft for attack on Pangkalan Brandan.

already very hot. The thoughtful Avenger stayed afloat long enough for us to get comfortable in the dinghy and then as if tired of life and with a few gurgles and hissing of steam, it sank.

Our first thought was to put as much distance between us and the land but the dinghy was difficult to move along. We felt sure that a boat would come out to pick us up. We only prayed that it would be the locals and that there were no Japs around. As time went on nothing happened from that direction and we began to get a bit of confidence but that wouldn't help us unless the Fleet sent someone in to look for us – and the Indian Ocean is a big expanse of sea. There was also the possibility of being found by the submarine posted up the coast for sea rescues. We saw the strike returning far above us and that made us feel very alone. My report written at the time tells the story:

REPORT BY LIEUT. (A) D.M. JUDD, R.N.V.R. ON DITCHING OF AVENGER 11C. JZ 554, 5 MILES OFF COAST OF SUMATRA ON 4TH JANUARY, 1945

Narrative
Having been airborne for 55 minutes with 849 Squadron from HMS Victorious on Operation 'Lentil', my engine cut almost completely. At this time the Strike was about 5 miles inland from Tapakyuan in Sumatra at 5000 feet, heading North East. I immediately pulled out of the formation and turned westward towards the sea and lost height. After 2 minutes it became inevitable that ditching would have to be carried out. I informed my crew to this effect and on crossing the coast, jettisoned my bomb load of 4 x 500 lb bombs. By this time the engine had cut completely; the aircraft was to all intents and purposes on fire, emitting clouds of white smoke from the engine, and filling the cockpit with fumes.

At 100 feet I dropped the flaps and carried out a water landing 5 miles from the coast. The actual landing produced no more shock than an average deck landing and the aircraft floated for 60 seconds before going under.

When I gave the ditching warning the Observer broadcast this fact on VHF giving the position and the Air Gunner broadcast it on H.F. and put the IFF to the emergency stop.

Ditching was carried out at 0805. The Air Gunner got out of the aircraft from the Turret Emergency Escape on the port side and immediately pulled out the dinghy. The Observer climbed out of the Centre Section on the starboard side and helped the Air Gunner with the dinghy. I got out of the aircraft on the port side, collected my jungle equipment which I thought might be useful during a long spell in the dinghy, and my K-type dinghy, and joined the Air Gunner.

Having climbed into the dinghy, our first thought was landwards. It was obvious, from the noise we had made coming down, the smoke trail we had left and our proximity to land, that we had been observed by the Japanese and/or the natives and that they would make some sort of attempt to capture us. Our most immediate task, therefore, was to put the oars into action and make every effort to make more distance between us and the land. This we did by taking turns with the oars in 10 minute shifts, in spite of a current running from our beam and our lack of skill in controlling the dinghy.

After 45 minutes of keeping one eye to landward and the other to seaward and rowing as hard as we could, 5 Hellcats arrived from the westward and just before reaching us, turned south and made for the coast 10 or 15 miles south of us. After 10 minutes they came northwards up the coast and appeared to be searching the beach. Our first reaction was to attract their attention with the various aids but declined from doing this for fear of attracting the Japanese as well. However, one Hellcat flew fairly close to us and we discharged a 'Signal Distress 2-star Mk. I' and he spotted us immediately.

The 5 Hellcats flew around us for some 10 minutes and then disappeared to our sorrow and nothing else was sighted for 30 minutes, during which time we began to give up hope and think that we might be there for some days till the ASR Submarine arrived. Then some Corsairs appeared from westward and repeated the same procedure as the Hellcats. Like the latter, they turned south and appeared to be searching the coast, beach and inland. They were too far away to attract their attention. However, soon one of them flew near us and we directed a Heliograph on to him and he spotted us.

Meanwhile two destroyers had been detached from the Fleet (unknown to us) and were making for a point on the coast some 20 miles south to search for us. Not finding us there, they steamed north and were finally directed on to us by the Corsair and our Heliograph. We were picked up about 10 miles from shore off Tapaktuan at 1125 by HMS 'Undine', whose boats crews did excellent work in double quick time.

Conclusions

(i)   We would never have been sighted by the Hellcats if it had not been for the 'Signal Distress 2-star Mk. I', which I consider invaluable.

(ii)   The Corsairs sighted the Heliograph reflection before they spotted the dinghy, having been flying in the vicinity between us and the shore for some 10 minutes. The destroyer saw the Heliograph long before they saw the dinghy and remarked on the brilliance of the light, and the assistance it gave them in spotting us.

(iii) When we were wondering whether the Japs would come out to get us before our own ships would arrive, the presence of our own aircraft overhead was a great reassurance, especially being fighters, as a guard against any boats or seaplanes coming to effect our capture.

(iv)   Although the length of time in the dinghy was comparatively short, one of the troubles I noticed and could see would be harmful, was sunstroke. At the time I didn't notice this but later became aware that the sun had had far more strength than I had then thought.

(v)   In the dinghy, we fell into a somewhat false sense of optimism whenever our own 'planes appeared and had a tendency to lean back and consider that we were all but picked up. Later we found that although we could see the fighters, they hadn't seen us; in fact the Corsairs were apparently giving up hope and were about to return to the carrier, when they saw the Heliograph signal. There definitely is a tendency to consider that a dinghy is an easy object to see from the air. In fact the chances of sighting a dinghy even from 1000 feet or less is very small unless some sort of distinctive signal is made from the dinghy – and no time should be wasted in making this signal.

Recommendations

(i)   In spite of the fact that 'Signal Distress 2-star Mk. I' are considered to be dangerous on 'Mae Wests', I suggest that the slight danger should be ignored and that all aircrews should carry at least four in their 'Mae Wests' as being about the best means of attracting attention of aircraft and ships, especially when cloudy conditions make the heliograph inoperative.

(ii) I suggest that a heliograph should also be carried in all 'Mae Wests' and that all dinghies should be supplied with them, for the same reason. They are small to stow and may save someone's life.

(iii) More than a dozen aircraft and two destroyers were used in this rescue. Much as we all appreciated the attention paid to us by the fighters and were thankful to see the destroyers, I consider that the job could have been done quite as successfully and far quicker by an ASR floatplane, attached to one of the cruisers or carriers, escorted by two fighters. Not only would the risk of sending destroyers away from the Fleet close inshore have been avoided, but an aircraft such as a Walrus is far more suited to searching for and spotting a dinghy than fighters, not only from the point of view of its speed but also owing to the number of 'eyes' it can carry.

(iv) I suggest that all aircraft dinghies ought to be equipped with a radio set for transmission of emergency signals. 2-8 star cartridges and heliographs are essential when the rescuers are in sight. But useless when no friendly aircraft or ship are around. This was borne out on this occasion when our own transmissions before ditching were not picked up by the carrier, with the result that delay was caused in sending a search craft.

(v)   Finally, the utmost importance should be attached in hot climate to covering the head from the sun. The effects of

Avenger going into the drink from HMS *Illustrious*.

Gone. (The crew were picked up.)

the sun are not noticed until it may be too late and sunstroke may result – a serious drawback when a long stay in a dinghy is ahead.

The sight of our fighters sent by Vian to find us cheered us up but they didn't spot us at the first sortie. Our spirits plummeted to the depths when they left us. The next flight looked everywhere except in our direction until they finally spotted us and then went away. Had they marked our position? As the following signal indicated, this was to be the last attempt to find us.

NAVAL MESSAGE
Undaunted, Undine (R) *Victorious*, D.25 R.A.A.

Proceed at utmost speed to position 03 degrees 17 N. 97 degrees 05 E. to recover 3 aircrew in dinghy.

Navigate with caution inshore.

8 Corsairs will escort you.

2. If Corsairs do not locate dinghy within ten minutes rejoin me in position 02 N. 96 53 E.

Indomitable will direct fighters. Keep guard on Admirals Wave.

0939

What joy it was when we spotted the two destroyers coming up the coast with an escort of fighters. The lead destroyer, HMS *Undine*, came near us, lowered a boat to pick us up and then we scrambled up the netting to the safety of the deck. The ship's medical officer was there to greet us, took us to a cabin for a thorough inspection. We were all shaking from shock but otherwise fit. Tea and brandy followed and a long long sleep. The ship's captain, Commander T.C. Robinson DSC and his crew were very welcoming and we had a relaxed journey back to Trincomalee. We transferred back to *Victorious* to a wonderful welcome and piss-up. We were grateful to Admiral Vian for his efforts to pick up one aircrew. We heard details of the attack that we had missed. It had been a very successful strike and plenty of damage had been done to the Pangkalan Brandan refinery. There had been little opposition and in fact we were the only casualties of the raid.

In some way or another, word got back to my family in England that I was missing, presumed killed.

NAVAL MESSAGE

To: *Victorious* (R) Admiralty   From: F.O. Air E.P.

IMPORTANT RESTRICTED

Following is a repetition of A.M. 022029

Begins unofficial information received by next of kin that Temp. Lieut. (A) D.T.Jodd repetition Jodd R.N.V.R. is missing presumed killed.

No repeat no information received Admiralty to this effect.

Request confirmation or otherwise urgently. Ends.

(2) Presume initials should read D.M. repeat D.M.

Request you will reply urgently.

10 1124 Z

Signals went backwards and forwards, eventually confirming that I was safe and well after the ducking off Sumatra.

A.J. McWhinnie, the First Naval Correspondent with the British Pacific Fleet wrote up the incident in the *Daily Herald* of 22nd February 1945 under the headline 'Saved from the Pacific'. He of course meant the Indian Ocean and we did not have to bale out but ditched the aircraft.

Saved From the Pacific

On one Eastern Fleet strike a British submarine became part of the Navy's Air-Sea Rescue Service by popping up at the right time near the enemy coast and rescuing airmen who had been forced into the sea.

During the recent Sumatra strike by the Fleet Air Arm from Eastern Fleet Forces, commanded by Vian, of *Cossack* fame, three Avenger bomber airmen were forced to bale out only three miles from the enemy coast. They clambered into their rubber dinghy, drifting behind a dangerous coral reef.

Despite the dangers, two destroyers were detailed by Admiral Vian to nose their way behind the reef and pick the airmen up. The destroyers brought all three men back alive.

That is the importance the Navy attaches to the lives of its flying men. Many of the lessons about bringing them back alive learned in the Indian Ocean will be acted upon in the Pacific.

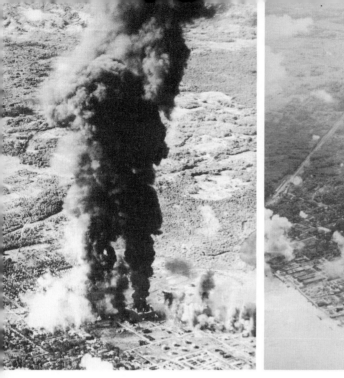

Attack on Pangkalan Brandan.

CHAPTER ELEVEN

Palembang

This was to be the preliminary skirmish to prepare the Fleet for greater things in the Pacific. Churchill had, so far at least, had his way in persuading the Americans that the British should join the attack on Japan from the Pacific theatre. Preparations had been going on for some time to bring the Fleeet to the required standard including a new aspect of British fleet operations – the Fleet Train. Distances were so great in the Pacific that it was impossible for the Fleet to return to base after every operation. The idea was that it would stay at sea for a month on end retreating from the battle zone when necessary to make a rendezvous with the Fleet Train. This consisted of oil and petrol tankers, ammunition ships, store ships and escort carriers carrying replacement aircraft and aircrew. Two days would be spent replenishing the Fleet which would then return to the battle zone for further operations.

All this took a lot of organisation but at last all was ready. The British Pacific Fleet was formed, the Fleet Train was ready and we finally left Ceylon on 16th January 1945. Lord Mountbatten, the Commander in Chief of South-East Asia Command, visited all the larger ships of the Fleet to address the officers and ships' companies to wish them well. His addresses were inspiring and confident and he gave a great boost to morale. The Fleet consisted of four carriers: *Indomitable* (Admiral Vian's flagship), *Illustrious*, *Victorious* and *Indefatigable*, together with the battleship *King George V*, four cruisers *Argonaut*, *Black Prince*, *Ceylon* and *Euryalus* and ten destroyers. It was the biggest concentration of carriers ever achieved by the Royal Navy. We were to make our way to Sydney, Australia, which was to be the rear base of the BPF but on the way we would be carrying out up to three strikes in quick succession against the two biggest oil refineries in the Far East, at Palembang in South-Eastern Sumatra. The Fleet's code name was Force 63.

This was to be the biggest series of operations ever carried out by the Fleet Air Arm in World War II, code named Meridian 1, 2 and 3. Palembang town lies on the north side of the Musi River, some miles from its mouth, south of Singapore and opposite Borneo. The two refineries were on the south bank of the river on either side of the Komerine river where it joins the Musi. Pladjoe which had been operated by Shell in peacetime lay on the north bank of the Komerine while Serongei Gerong was on the opposite bank. The confluence of the rivers, the town and the huge refineries, all within an area of five miles was to make spotting them easy. Their size was to make the obliteration of these targets highly important in denying much needed oil to the Jap forces.

The carriers carried 238 aircraft made up of Hellcats, Corsairs, Avengers, Fireflies, Seafires and two air-rescue Walruses.

Before we left Trincomalee, we took part in a rehearsal attack on Colombo by all four carrier groups. The day after we put to sea on 16th January, Commander Owen, our Commander Operations, called the senior officers of the *Victorious* squadrons to the operations room to tell us about the immediate future.

'Well, boys,' he said, 'we are making for Sydney and up to the Pacific as the British Pacific Fleet. But on the way we will be knocking hell out of two oil refineries at Palembang.' He then described where they were and what they were at the same time removing the dust sheet from the large model of the two refineries and the surrounding land. The model was perfect in every detail. 'Well, there it is – there will be at least one attack on each refinery and if necessary a third to mop up anything that has been left undamaged. Now go along and tell your aircrews and work out a plan. You may come in here to study the model at any time and make sure you know it like the back of your hand. From now on we shall get together every day and all day to perfect plans and ensure that everyone knows his job to the last detail. But I warn you, there will be stiff opposition from ack-ack and fighters. That's all for the moment.'

For the next few days, we talked, dreamt and thought nothing but Palembang. I can't say it was exciting. We all began to get rather tense as the immensity of the task and the likely opposition sank in. We were each given specific targets within the refineries. Mine was

Admiral Lord Mountbatten (2nd. from right) with Captain Denny (far right) HMS *Victorious*.

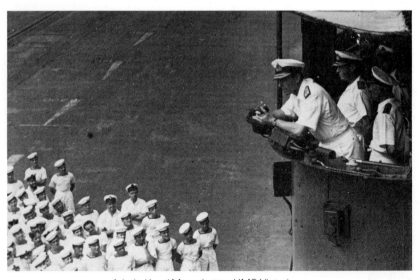

Admiral Lord Mountbatten HMS *Victorious*.

one of the cracking plants. The first one at Pladjoe was on a crossroads in the centre of the refinery and was therefore not difficult to pin-point – at least on the model.

'On no account hit the storage tanks. If you do, they will catch fire, belch black smoke and put a blanket over the target.'

This is what happened in fact, except that the smoke fortunately didn't hover low over the target area. The reported opposition filled us with terror.

'There are signs of heavy concentrations of heavy and light ack ack at the target and you must be prepared for a heavy barrage. The target is also protected by quite a lot of good fighter squadrons and you must be prepared to be jumped as you approach, in your dive and during the get-away to the rendezvous as well as returning home. But you'll have plenty of fighter cover from the Hellcats and Corsairs.'

Someone asked if there were likely to be any balloons.

'No, aerial reconnaissance doesn't show any balloons.' This was, to our horror, to prove very wrong in the event.

Victorious was to provide twelve Avengers of 849 Squadron to make up No 1 Bomber Wing with the leading squadron – 857 from *Indomitable* led by 'Doc' Stuart. The second Bomber Wing consisted of Avengers of 854 Squadron from *Illustrious* and 820 Squadron from *Indefatigable*. We were all armed with four 500 lb bombs. Top and middle cover was provided by Corsairs and Hellcats and close cover was provided by Fireflies. The Air-Co-ordinator was Major 'Ronnie' Hay from *Victorious*. The whole operation involved 140 aircraft. 849 was to fly in the usual two stepped down formations of six aircraft each; David Foster leading the first and I the second.

We were due to make the first strike against Pladjoe refinery on 22nd January, the flying-off position being between Engano Island and the coast of South Sumatra. But I for one was pretty tensed up with apprehension for the success of the flight itself with so many aircraft involved and me responsible for five other crews; fear for the opposition we should certainly meet and scared stiff at the thought of falling into the hands of this particular enemy. These emotions were not helped by our meeting appalling weather during the night of 21/22nd which caused a 24 hour delay. That didn't do the nerves any good. Flying was quite out of the question as we met a prolonged tropical storm of high winds and driving rain. Back again the next morning but the weather was no better. Another withdrawal and another run into the flying position of a take-off on the 24th. The wind had dropped and the rain stopped but there was low cloud over the fleet. Would we, wouldn't we? What anxious moments in anxious days those were with that awful fear of the unknown with the inevitability of dangers ahead with frightening results.

Presently, we were put out of our misery. The tannoy blared 'Stand by to fly off aircraft' and so it was on. This was at 0500 with take-off at 0630. An agonizing 90 minutes to wait.

The take-off was without incident but the form up was a shambles underneath a low cloud ceiling of about 1000 feet. Round and round the fleet we went chasing each other's tails, till I felt like saying, 'For Christ's sake, get on with it.'

Eventually we did and made for the coast underneath the cloud. And then a bit of luck for the cloud dispersed, the coast was clear and the morning bright. We had to climb fast for the coast to clear the 11,000 foot Barisan Range of mountains. No problems this time although I couldn't help thinking of the last time I tried to climb mountains hanging on my prop. We made it to 13,000 feet and there, in other circumstances, was a lovely sight of the lush green of the Sumatran plain and beyond it the misty blue of sea of the Bangka Straits and the South China Sea beyond. Come on, this is no time to enjoy the view. And no sooner thought but there were the rivers – and Palembang – and the two vast refineries just where the model said they would be. My God, what a size they are.

And then all hell was let loose. Radio silence had been maintained up to that point but now the ether was filled with shouting. It started with an excited voice bawling, 'Rats, 10 o'clock up,' then the babble became quite unintelligible, like turning on the wireless at full blast with three stations on or near the same wavelength. I saw two of the rats screaming down on us and thought, 'Christ, the party has started early.' The bomber wing leader started letting down to increase speed and weaving. Another horror of horrors; what were those brown sausage looking things just above the target. There must be a dozen of them and they were climbing. Oh! Lord, they are balloons which aren't supposed to be here. And clearly they are ready for us.

Screaming fighters, theirs and ours were all over the place. Two of theirs got through the cover and were attacking us – my observer, George was giving me a running commentary but they broke away without scoring any hits. Nearing the target now and the heavy ack-ack was opening up. Shell bursts galore just in front and very slightly below us, the brown puffs of smoke passing us in a flash – they can stay there, I thought. There was the target on the starboard side in the angle of the engine cowling and the wing. Come on, let's go, it's getting too hot up here and I feel very naked. Good, there we go and the wing leader peels off to starboard and down, followed by his Avengers. OK, there's the cracking plant at Padjoe, no difficulty in seeing it but it looked a small target to hit. There goes David Foster and his flight. Now me and mine. We were in the perfect position for the dive from 10,500 feet. Got through the heavy barrage OK. Now the balloons. Hell, what do I do. The balloons were obvious – big floating innocuous-looking brown sausages with red circles on the side of them. Nobody was shooting them down. But it was the cables that were the worry and I couldn't see any cables. All I knew was that the cables didn't go down to the ground vertically but in a loop. Down to 7,000 feet and they were dashing up to meet us. 250 – 280 – 300 knots. Can't do anything about the balloons but just hope. Check bomb doors open, finger on release button on stick. Eyes fixed on damn cracking plant getting bigger by the split second.

Through the balloons and now the light ack-ack opened up. Tracer cut through the sky all around. Up to 320 knots and down to 4000 feet. Will release bombs at 2,500. Didn't have to look at the altimeter as I knew what things looked like at 2,500 ft from long practice. Here we go, press the tit and feel the plane lift as the bombs go. Pull back hard on the stick and nearly black out but the speed of the plane takes us clear over the main river.

George yells out over the inter-com 'You've hit it – a real beauty right on the nail.'

I couldn't see our handiwork but there were things to think of. Kept on three quarters throttle and increased the pitch. Had to get to that rendezvous which meant a left hand turn round the target. God, here comes the tracer again. Hell, it's accurate and intense; weaved and bobbed to shake them off. This was from the neighbourhood of the town of Palembang. Then a strange thing happened. For a split second, I couldn't believe it. I looked out the starboard side and there was a sleek twin-engined Jap fighter – a Nick – sitting on my starboard wing and almost touching me. The two pilots were looking at me with their sickly grin – the bastards. They couldn't shoot at me from there and it was just occurring to me that they were going to ram me or tip my wing, when the Nick burst into flames, keeled over to starboard and made for the ground out of control and blazing. Thank God, two less little bastards.

Now, come on, concentrate, it's not over yet. Where is the rendezvous? George was conning me on to the right direction and height. We had to climb to a pre-ordered height. Where is everyone? The sky seemed suddenly empty except for the storage tanks which were throwing up masses of black smoke which covered the target but made it look like a spectacular attack. Oh, good, there is an Avenger and another and a third wheeling around. Climbed to meet them and joined up in a loose formation. More began to join in as we set course for home.

No time to waste, petrol consumption had to be thought of and there was a good 150 miles to go; up over the mountains and, how wonderful, there was the sea and hopefully the Fleet. Will my engine last for the last two laps? Seems all right and oil pressure and temperature normal. Began to feel elated as we let down to 2,500 feet over the sea. There they are but where is *Victorious?* Will probably land on the wrong carrier. Don't care after all that. We sort ourselves out over the fleet. Find Vic and fly down starboard side for the sweep round to port for the landing on. Will the undercarriage go down. Good, it's OK, fine pitch, flaps down, hook down. Turn in to land thinking of that pint waiting for me. Mouth is dry, arse is sore and tiredness is setting in. It is still only 0930.

Land on successfully and roar forward over the lowered barrier to forward lift, cut engine, fold wings and get out with very wobbly legs. I'm nearly sick. The ground crew are obviously delighted to see us. We head for a long detailed debriefing in the Ops Room. And then that pint and the best breakfast I'd had for a long time. Everybody's talking at once about experiences. There is an air of elation in the wardroom since we all know we've made a success of it.

It had been in fact a great success but there was to be a second

First attack on Palembang.

Climbing over mountains in Sumatra.

attack on the other refinery at Soengei Gerong and perhaps a third to hit any missed targets. This thought was sobering. However, all Vic's aircrew had returned though the Fleet had lost nine aircraft and many were damaged.

The Fleet had to withdraw for refuelling. This was somewhat of a shambles due to inexperience. However, from our point of view, the refuelling was an awful waste of time and bad on the nerves. I wouldn't have minded so much if we could have gone in again next day but a five day wait to carry out Meridian 2 was hard on the nerves. Furthermore, information trickled through that the Japs knowing that another attack was almost certainly imminent because the other refinery had been left untouched were strengthening their defences and that in particular they were bringing down from the north some crack fighter squadrons to augment the local squadrons.

The refuelling period was used to examine in detail the faults shown up in the first operation in Pladjoe. The destruction of the balloons was the first priority and fighter dispositions were altered to achieve this. Secondly and more important, the flight path from target to rendezvous was revised. Instead of turning to port around the town of Palembang with all its flak, it was decided to leave the target to starboard and go round the south and west to the rendezvous.

Finally, it was 849's turn to lead one group of the bombers and this was to prove fatal to the squadron in view of the fact that there would be no surprise this time. We all knew that they would be waiting for us – fighters with their now experienced squadrons, heavy and light flak and balloons.

This time, 849 Squadron's targets at the Soengei Gerong refinery were the Redistillation unit and Fractionating columns.

We were back at the flying-off position by the evening of the 29th. In the meantime the ground crews had worked like beavers to get the planes repaired and ready for further action. Night and day they worked in the hot and sweaty atmosphere of the hangar deck under fierce arc lights. But they succeeded and twelve Avengers were ranged for Meridian 2. The weather at first light on the 29th was appalling; low cloud and rain and a swell made conditions for take-off and forming up near to impossible. But take off we did and the form up was remarkably good. We took off at 0650 and in spite of the poor visibility, set course for Palembang half an hour later. 849 was leading and we were under no illusions as to what we were in for. Fortunately, the weather improved as we crossed the mountains at 13,000 feet. But the pattern of the operation was soon to manifest itself. The Jap fighters were up in force and were attacking us by the time we got over the plain of Sumatra and with nearly 100 miles to go. There were to be continuous air battles all the way to the target when the heavy ack ack took over. And there were those bloody balloons. Some were shot down this time, but there were plenty guarding the refinery. We were attacked again and again by fighters, the most severe one being just short of the target and this attack caused sad losses to the squadron. The ack ack was more accurate too than the first time. The heavies were uncomfortably close and intense.

There was the target and down we went through the balloons. I was committed to the dive and had got under the balloons when I saw two Avengers on my port side diving along side me. Suddenly they both hit balloon cables which tore off their wings, and they went down to certain death out of control. One of them was Lieutenent-Commander Mainprice, the CO of 854 Avenger Squadron from *Illustrious*. How dreadful to watch but it was no good thinking one's thoughts. At 320 knots and hurtling through balloon cables in the middle of intense flak, it was everyone for himself. Christ, this is terrible – what an inferno. Down to 4,000 feet and a bit to go. 2,500 feet and lined up on target. I lift the nose slightly and press the tit – bombs gone, thank God. How to get out of this hell. Pull back the stick and hard rudder to starboard.

George on inter-com: 'We've done it again – the bombs were smack in the centre of the target.'

I was pleased but had other things on my mind. We were being jumped by fighters again. Oh God, where are our fighters? Once again I feel alone with an awful long way to the rendezvous. We jerk and weave and fly low and fast to get out of it and after the hurtling dive at over 300 the climb to the rendezvous seemed slow.

We reach the rendezvous by 0900 and waste no time in setting course for home. But where is everyone? There are many missing from 849 Squadron. This is worse than last time. Who have gone down? Apart from the two who had hit the balloon cables, I had seen one of my Avengers hit and downed by a burst of heavy flak; two or three had been damaged. A Jap fighter had gone down in flames and one of our fighters had crashed near the target. Two more Avengers were shot down by fighters on the way to the rendezvous and others had been damaged. What an appalling carnage.

It was a much reduced squadron that started its long flight home. We were all worried as to whether we would make it over the mountains and home to the Vic. Those who had been damaged could only hope. The engines had been treated harshly and had really taken a hammering. Overheating was the main problem but we were being jumped constantly by Jap fighters as they followed us out. Then we had to climb to 11,000 feet again to get over the mountains. I felt my engine complaining and I began to wonder whether I would make it.

The crossing of the mountains came as a relief – it was downhill from there on so the engine could be nursed. The sea was in sight too and then that lovely sight of the Fleet waiting for us. Please God, don't ask me to come here again. We, or those of us left, made it to the carriers thankful beyond words to touch down and catch the welcoming wire on the Flight Deck. I got out of the plane on the forward lift. A quick look round the deck and the circuit and I could only count six planes out of the twelve that had left three hours before. I nearly fainted with fear for the others. My legs were like jelly as I made my way to the Ops Room.

That afternoon, the Fleet was attacked by seven low flying bombers thought at first to be torpedo planes but turned out to be suicide bombers. They were all shot down by Seafires and ships' guns without achieving any success.

Seven planes from 849 were lost over the two operations and ten of their total of nineteen aircraft were lost or unserviceable. In the second attack four crews were missing and one observer died from wounds received over the target. We were the hardest hit of all the carriers. Overall the Fleet lost 41 aircraft from 380 sorties and thirty aircrew were lost including nineteen Avenger aircrew. A very high price to pay. But it was judged to be a most successful operation and the loss of oil to the Japs was a very real factor in future operations in the Pacific. Production ceased for two months and thereafter the two refineries were working at only a third of capacity.

Second attack on Palembang.

Kamikaze attack on fleet after Palembang.

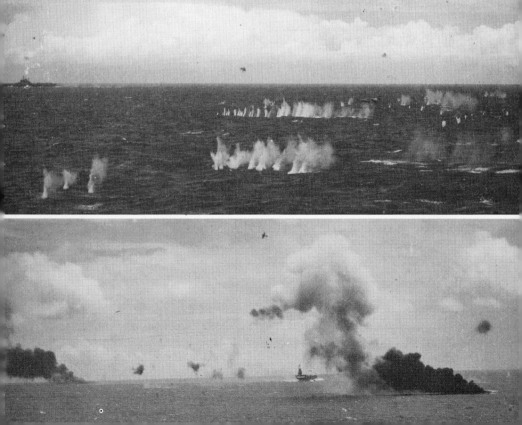

However, all was not over yet. We were due to carry out Meridian 3 next morning. How many planes 849 could have had ready by then was doubtful and the nerves of the pilots had worn thin. I dread to think of the consequences. I believe the casualties would have been appalling. I spent the morning in a state of gloom about the next day but busy worrying about the state of the aircraft and how many we were likely to have available. Then, at midday the tannoy blared out: 'Meridian 3 has been cancelled. The Fleet is proceeding to Sydney, Australia.' I felt as if a ton weight had been lifted from me and the relief was indescribable. There was unbelieving relief showing in all the faces of the aircrew.

My emotions were made more frail by the loss of some good friends. Gunn, an observer in 849, died from wounds as his pilot ditched after abortive attempts at landing on Vic. Gus Halliday and Pattison ditched too but were picked up by a destroyer. But Ken Burrenston, Lintern, Burns and Roebuck were shot down over the target. They all survived and were taken prisoners but, poor fellows, were not to live. Burrenston and Lintern and at least seven other survivors were taken from their prisoner of war camp after the surrender of Japan on 15th August 1945. They were lined up and brutally murdered by the camp commandant cutting off their heads with a ceremonial sword. The murderers were brought to justice and paid the price with their lives. I was sick when news of these atrocities filtered through after the war. Memories of such things remain always vivid, always bitter.

CHAPTER TWELVE

The Pacific

So, it was with a sense of utmost relief that we left the target area and made for Fremantle, Western Australia, where we arrived on 4th February. In the meantime I had flown over to the *Indomitable* taking with me the Air Coordinator, Ronnie Hay, Lieutenant-Commander Tomkinson, the CO of 1836, the Corsair squadron and Lieutenant-Commander Hopkins, the CO of 1834 Corsair Squadron. We went up to the Admiral's bridge where all the other senior squadron officers from the other carriers were meeting. This was a high powered de-briefing and discussion on the two Palembang operations. What was achieved, what went wrong, lessons to be learnt for future operations in the Pacific were all discussed with candour. Vian encouraged everyone to talk, to air their views and be as critical of the overall plan for which he was responsible as well as the carrying out of it for which the squadron commanders were responsible.

No holds were barred and as a result many faults were examined to see what could be done to improve future operations. There was a long way to go as eventual contact with the American Task forces was to show but it would be fair to say that the British Pacific Fleet and the Air Group began to grow up into the new concept of a fast, efficient and hard hitting Task Force with, if necessary, continuous flying that was a feature of the American naval operations in the Pacific. The idea of the one set piece strike was to give way to constant take-offs and landings by smaller numbers of strike aircraft and continuous streams of fighters as circumstances demanded.

After refuelling and replenishing, the Fleet set sail for Australia and a welcome run ashore to Perth but we only stayed for a day or so before sailing through the roaring forties to Sydney. Unfortunately, I was detailed to take six of the 849 Avengers ashore to Royal Naval Air Station Nowra some seventy miles south of

One way to land on a carrier.

Another way to land on carrier.

HMS *Victorious* in Sydn Harbour.

Sydney. It was not a very attractive station but it did provide a change from shipboard life. Apart from trips to Jervis Bay and up to Sydney and back, we did little but relax. A week later we flew up to Mascot Airfield outside Sydney and rejoined the ship before going on five days' leave. What a sight Sydney Harbour was. It was so big that the BPF with all its ships was lost in it. No wonder the Aussies boasted of 'Our 'arbour, our bridge, our Bradman.' And the welcome we got was embarrassing. And news of the Palembang success which had preceded us made the celebrations even greater. The four carriers certainly rode proudly at anchor in the harbour for the eighteen days we were there.

My first run ashore was, however, disappointing in the extreme. A few of us caught the 5 pm liberty boat dressed up for an evening on the town. We would for a start make for the Hotel Australia in the centre of the city to get there as the bar opened at six – or so we thought. We arrived on the dot only to find the bar closing, the lights being turned out and the hotel resembling a morgue, dark, empty and no one about to help us. No one had told us the peculiarities of the New South Wales licensing laws.

'No, you can't get a drink after six, mate. No, there is no food in the evening – not much point as the City empties and everyone goes home.' What a let down. That evening was one of the war's failures but we soon learnt and invitations came flooding in for trips to Bondi Beach and Manley, parties at the homes of Australians especially along the beautiful harbour coast in Rose Bay, Elizabeth Bay and Vercluse. We were made so welcome and felt that we had earned the luxurious living after the trauma of Palembang and before the future action in the Pacific. It gave us a much needed and very enjoyable breathing space.

But it had to end and on 9th February we left Sydney for the north and the Pacific arriving at Manus in the Admiralty Islands on 7th March, carrying out big exercises all the way there. Up past the Great Barrier Reef, through the Coral Sea, past the eastern tip of New Guinea; getting hotter and hotter all the time. We began to feel what it was like to be in the tropics again, in our cabins way down in the bowels of the ship and under that heat-attracting steel flight deck. Manus was a huge anchorage. The weather was hot and humid with every so often big tropical storms sweeping across the area which turned day into night and the heavens opened to torrential rain blown by hurricane type winds. A shirt was wet through with perspiration in no time and that happened while you were just sitting still. The whole atmosphere was debilitating in the extreme.

For the first time, I realised the sheer size of the Pacific, the vastness of the water with little in it save small islands and atolls scattered about with hundreds of miles between them. I had been looking forward to seeing the Pacific and its Coral Islands and reefs. Like many others of my age I had been brought up on books about the Pacific Islands and they had fired my imagination. I never expected to see them in reality but here I was among them all. And what a let down it was. They were so disappointing. The youthful dreams of adventure and exploration among the coral reefs melted as quickly as ice-cream under the tropical sun. It was like the fantasy of a mirage.

Water was rationed in the tropics, especially as the Fleet Train was anchored some way away from us. Fresh food from Australia gave way to tinned food and the inevitable dull diet. And on top of this, as if that wasn't bad enough, there followed an argument between the top politicians as to the role of the BPF resulting in the Fleet being stuck at Manus for ten days with nothing to do but to wait and wait day after day. This whole episode did nothing to give us any confidence in politicians, especially the American variety. In a nutshell, the problem was quite simple; Churchill wanted a British Navy presence in the Pacific to assist in the defeat of the Japs. The Commander in Chief of the United States Fleet, Admiral King, whose dislike of the British was well known, did not want the British Navy anywhere near the Pacific. Negotiations over the role of the BPF had been long and difficult but at least the Fleet had been formed and other principles agreed between the two countries. The Commander in Chief of the British Pacific Fleet, Admiral Fraser, had gone to Pearl Harbour to meet and discuss the subject with Admiral Nimitz.

All was organised and we had been on our way from the beginning of the year to fight alongside the American Task Force in the Central Pacific. We were to join in Operation Iceberg, designed to capture Okinawa from the Japs as a stepping stone to the eventual invasion

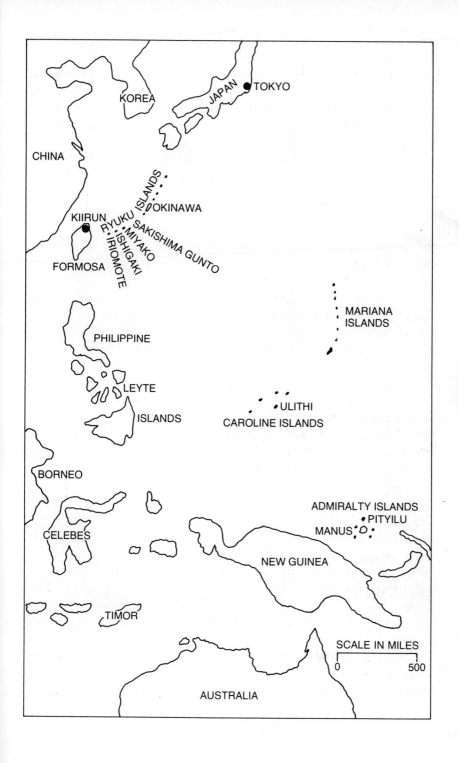

KOREA

CHINA

JAPAN

TOKYO

RYUKU ISLANDS

OKINAWA

KIIRUN

SAKISHIMA GUNTO

MIYAKO

ISHIGAKI

IRIOMOTE

FORMOSA

MARIANA
ISLANDS

PHILIPPINE

LEYTE

ISLANDS

ULITHI

CAROLINE ISLANDS

BORNEO

ADMIRALTY ISLANDS

PITYILU

MANUS

CELEBES

NEW GUINEA

TIMOR

SCALE IN MILES

0   500

AUSTRALIA

In the Pacific.

Mail being delivered at sea off Okinawa.

of Japan itself. Admiral King did not want the BPF to join the American 5th Fleet under Admiral Spruance which was to carry out the naval operation against Okinawa. He wanted us to stay in the south Pacific in a minor role employed in the planned invasion of Borneo.

King's objections were eventually overcome but not before morale and spirits in the BPF became very low indeed, not least among the aircrew. Admiral Vian tried to keep our spirits up by ordering a practice strike and sending planes ashore to Pityilu airfield. I took 849 there ostensibly for more flying practice but the conditions were so appalling that our morale plunged even lower. I remember one plan was for a night attack from Pityilu on the fleet, a conventional dive-bombing strike from 10,000 feet. I didn't fancy that for a start and we were saved by a tropical storm brewing up at dusk. In no way did I want to risk the whole squadron getting mixed up in one of those storms at night and I managed to get through to the Fleet and obtained permission to cancel the exercise. However, the visit to Pityilu showed us two things. One was the immensity of the American resources and the efficiency with which they got a base going so soon after capture. Although Manus was rough and uncomfortable and far removed from the popular idea of a South Pacific Island, it was in working order only a week or so after being captured by the Americans.

The other interesting thing that I came across for the first time at Pityilu was a runway made entirely of coral. The airfield had only one runway but it was a long and wide one. The coral had been bulldozed and rolled to form a white shiny strip. It was in fact highly disconcerting particularly in landing on it. From the approach, it gave the impression of a long skating rink. Dazzlingly white and slightly wet, one's reaction was to land 'gingerly' and with no use of the brakes. Fortunately its length and width made the use of brakes unnecessary and one only prayed for a stable landing with no swing. This was not always easy in tropical conditions in which the wind could very quickly change its direction and strength. I don't think I ever put it to the test but I was glad to get back to the arrester wires of the carrier.

So after a complete waste of ten days while the politicians argued, King relented and we received the news to set sail for Ulithi in the

Caroline Islands. We left the God-forsaken Manus on 17th March arriving at Ulithi on the 20th. Ulithi was a huge coral reef forming a vast natural harbour. Every now and again round the reef the coral would emerge above the sea to form a ring of islands. They were uninhabited, almost treeless and hundreds of miles from anywhere. We were able to refuel there. And on 23rd March we sailed from Ulithi as Task Force 57 to join the Americans in the recapture of Okinawa. We came under the overall command of Admiral Nimitz at Honolulu and more immediately his second in command, Admiral Spruance.

The British Pacific Fleet was assigned the task of neutralising the airfield on the islands forming the Sakishima Gunto part of the Ryukyu Islands in support of the American landings in Okinawa lying to the north-east. It was thought that the Japs would seek to replenish their Air Force on Okinawa by flying planes in from China by way of Formosa and the islands of the Sakishima Gunto. The three main islands were Iriomote, Ishigaki, and Miyako, all with airfields and our job was to put and then keep airfields unusable and thus stop the supply of aircraft to Okinawa.

The fleet consisted of two battleships, *King George V*, the flagship, and *Howe*; four carriers; *Indomitable*, *Illustrious*, *Victorious* and *Indefatigable*, four cruisers and a number of destroyers. *Victorious* carried fourteen Avengers, thirty-seven Corsairs and two Walruses for sea rescue duties.

The general plan was that the Fleet would make for a flying-off position some 100 miles from the three islands. From there the four carrier groups of bombers and fighters would keep up a continuous attack on the islands from dawn to dusk as circumstances demanded. The Avengers would go in always at dawn and dusk and sometimes in between to drop bombs on the runways so that they could not be used by the enemy and would attack any other worthwhile targets like airfield installations and aircraft. The usual force was between three and six bombers variously spread over the islands and perhaps attacking two in succession. Attacks were by the conventional dive bombing techniques. The fighters would be used to protect the bombers or to carry out independent strafing of the airfields. Fighters would also maintain a constant air cover above the Fleet. The result was a continuous round of ranging up on deck,

Take off for attack on Formosa.

Off the Sakishima Gunto.

take-off, landing back on the carrier from before first light to darkness. Behind this deck work was the constant maintenance of aircraft round the clock in the stifling and humid conditions of the hangar deck. The Fleet could not operate for more than three days at the flying off positions. At the end of that period it would withdraw some 200 miles to meet the Fleet Train where it would stay for anything between one and three days to take on fuel for the ships, petrol for the aircraft, food, stores, mail and replacement aircraft and aircrew, the latter from the escort carriers attached to the Fleet Train. Then the Fleet would return to the flying off position for a further three day stint. This programme was to last for nearly a month before we all returned to Leyte in the Philippines for a rest, replenishment and repairs. Aircrews would be relieved and new ones take over. The dead would be buried at sea from the carrier, the injured would be transferred to hospital ships at the refuelling point and finally to better equipped hospital ships at Leyte at the end of the month.

Nobody fancied these operations. In spite of constant attention from our bombers and fighters, the airfields continued to be strongly defended and the ack ack particularly was heavy and accurate. Losses were heavy, ditchings regular and prangs constant. Boredom at bombing the runways day in and day out set in early. And frustration too, as it was obvious very early on that the craters caused by the day's attacks were filled in that night. This required daily attention to create more craters only for them to be filled in again and so on. Day by day morale deteriorated as losses and crashes mounted just for the sake of displacing earth for it to be replaced in a matter of hours. The following reports that I made on two of the operations tell the story of these attacks:

OPERATION 'ICEBERG'
2nd Strike – 26th March, 1945 – Strike "DOG"
REPORT BY LT. (A) D.M. JUDD, R.N.V.R.,

849 SQUADRON
1220 Airborne
1246 Set course for target
1330 Attacked Nobara Airfield on Miyako Jima
1336 Set course from rendezvous

1400 Attacked Miyara Airfield on Ishigaki Jima
1410 Set course from rendezvous
1502 Over "Tomcat"
1550 Landed
Owing to the absence of *Indefatigable* Avengers, 849 Flight, consisting of 6 aircraft, formed up on the port quarter of Strike Leader's flight. Strike proceeded to target without incident, climbing to 10,000 feet.

2.   Over the target, 7/10 cumulus cloud from 4,000 – 6,000 feet was encountered; I took the flight through the cloud to bomb the airfield installations at Nobara Airfield from SE – NW. Bombs were seen to drop on runways, dispersals and AA positions. No aircraft were seen on the airfield. Little and inaccurate AA opposition was encountered.

3.   The Strike rendezvous and climbed to 8,000 feet on the way to second target – Miyara Airfield on Ishigaki. Owing to cloud over this island at 6,000 – 7,500 feet, Strike let down to cloud base and flew round airfield to bomb W. – E. Bombs were seen to drop on intersection of runways, dispersals and buildings.

4.   Moderate heavy AA fire was encountered from direction of Ishigaki Airfield. This was fairly accurate due to the Strike flying immediately below cloud base before 'pushing over'.

5.   No enemy aircraft were airborne over either target.

6.   It is considered that the forming up before and at the rendezvous was slow on both occasions. This might have caused the loss of one or two aircraft if any interceptors had been waiting on the way to the rendezvous.
29th March 1945   Lieut. (A) RNVR

*

OPERATION 'ICEBERG'
2nd Strike – 27th March, 1945 – Strike 'CHARLIE'
REPORT BY LT. (A) D.M. JUDD R.N.V.R., 849 SQUADRON
1230 Airborne

1245 Set course for target
1332 Attacked Sukama Airfield on Miyako Jima
1337 Set course for rendezvous
1415 Set course for base
1423 Jettisoned bombs
1435 Over 'Jigsaw'
1452 Over 'Tomcat'
1530 Landed
849 flight of 4 aircraft formed the Green Flight of the 2nd
Squadron.

2.   The Strike climbed to 9,500 feet through a thin layer of
9/10 cloud at 8,500 – 9,000 feet. The Strike orbited
Miyako Jima above the cloud, deployed in line astern and
were ordered to drop one bomb on Sukama Airfield.
During the long approach dive from SE – NW slight
heavy AA from batteries near Nobara and Hirara
Airfields was encountered.

3.   Bombs were seen to drop on runways, ammunition store,
barracks and dispersals.

4.   The Strike rendezvoused and climbed to 5,000 feet, but
between Tarama Jima and Ishigaki Jima thick storm
clouds prevented approach at that height and the Strike
turned and let down to 800 feet. A second approach to
Ishigaki Jima was made at 800 feet from the East but it
was obvious that the weather was too bad over the island
and after a search of the coast for shipping, the Strike set
course for base. Eight minutes later, on orders from the
Strike leader, the bombers deployed and jettisoned the
remaining bomb load into the sea.

5.   It is surprising that the Group Commander, having seen
that the weather was impossible over Ishagaki Jima; did
not order the Strike to return to Miyako and drop the
remaining bombs on one of the airfields there. If,
however, the targets at Miyako did not warrant a return
there, the wastage of bombs in the sea appears
unnecessary in view of the fact that the bombs carried
were quite safe with which to carry out a deck landing.

29th March, 1945   LIEUT. (A) RNVR

Loss of morale, loss of friends, our efforts never likely to show any finality and the heat and sweat and the round the clock maintenance, organization and management of the daily strikes took its toll. This caused carelessness, bloody mindedness, boredom and frustration which didn't help the accident rate. And a month at sea in those conditions was not pleasant. I don't think we ever did close down the airfields and if that was so, was it worth the attention of Task Force 57, its Fleet Train, over 200 aircraft for a month on end ... and all the losses of men and aircraft that we suffered? I doubt it.

We did have a welcome break when we were ordered to bomb airfields in Formosa, an operation called Iceberg Oolong. We made for the flying-off position between the Sakishima Gunto and Formosa arriving on 11th April. But the weather was bad and the attack was postponed for 24 hours. 849 was assigned to Matsuyama airfield but on arrival, it was closed in by weather so we made for the alternative target of Kiirun harbour. There was no fighter opposition but the flak was heavy. Nevertheless we successfully attacked harbour installations and shipping, making our get away through the valleys to the south and east. We were glad to have something positive to attack and see the results though we were sad to lose one of our crews who didn't return.

There was another aspect of war in the Pacific and that was the dreaded Kamikaze. The first attack by one of these was on 1st April when, amid a lot of enemy activity over the Fleet, a Kamikaze dived at *Indefatigable* with its 500 lb bomb and crashed on the flight deck by the island superstructure. Much damage was caused and casualties in dead and wounded were heavy but in less than an hour the flight deck was operational. Here was demonstrated the advantage of the British carrier with its armoured deck over the American counterpart with its wooden deck. A Kamikaze hitting an American carrier in its flight deck would penetrate to the hangar deck causing immense damage and putting the carrier out of action for a long time.

Later, *Victorious* tasted such an attack. The Jap plane dived on the ship. Captain Denny was turning to starboard but on seeing the Jap, he increased the speed of the turn. The pilot tried to correct his approach but had obviously committed himself to the attack and missed. It did strike its wing tip on the edge of the flight deck on the port side but dived into the sea where the bomb blew up harmlessly with a hell of a bang. Bits of the aircraft were thrown on to the deck along with a mass of water but no remains of the pilot.

For me personally, the month or two up to the end of the first series of operations at Sakishima Gunto were pretty miserable. I shared of course the dislike of the area and the type of operations we were called upon to undertake, as well as the sadness at what I regarded as unnecessary losses and accidents. But by then, there were other factors having a bearing on my morale. Of course, fear was ever present but I began to get twitchy and a feeling of premonition that something was going to happen (an imagination that, thank God, didn't materialise). Fear is normal and perhaps necessary like, in a different sphere and different degree, pre-concert nerves. But twitchiness and an over active imagination is dangerous and can lead to mistakes, bad judgement and poor leadership. I think I must have begun to get tired after nearly four years continuously in operational squadrons. Perhaps it was the reaction of the ditching at Pankalan Brandan followed immediately by the costly attacks at Palembang and the loss of so many friends.

It was made worse by a personal sadness. After we left Manus, I began to hear news that my father was ill. But there were four letters from home which didn't reach me till weeks later. And I was ten thousand miles away and couldn't just phone up from mid Pacific. By the time we got to Sakishimo it appeared that his illness was more serious than I had at first thought and I started worrying. Finally, a letter telling me that he had died – weeks before. The news shattered me coming relatively soon after my mother's death and catching me when I was at a low ebb anyway. After the last operation on 20th April when I attacked Nobara airfield on Miyako for the last time, we finally withdrew to Leyte for a rest to everyone's relief. On the way Captain Denny called for me to see him on the bridge.

'Ah, Judd,' he said, taking me on one side. 'I am going to send you home; I think you've done enough. I want to thank you for all you have done in *Victorious*. *Illustrious* is leaving the Task Force at Leyte and I am arranging for you to take passage in her to Sydney. Good luck ... Oh, and I am so sorry to hear about your father.'

HMS *Formidable* hit by Kamikaze.

Kamikaze attack on *Victorious* off Okinawa, taken from *Illustrious*.

Illustrious in dry dock Sydney.

I began packing up with much relief. I felt I just couldn't face another spell off the Sakishima Gunto and whatever was to follow. A farewell party in the wardroom at Leyte and a picnic on the beach and a final goodbye to that happy ship *Victorious* and all my friends in 849 Squadron as I was taken over by boat to *Illustrious*. There I joined Norman Hanson and his Corsair boys and 854 Avenger crews who were going home with the ship. I was to disembark at Sydney to fly back to the UK.

Illustrious left Leyte on 3rd May for Sydney via Manus arriving in Sydney on 14th May. The only incident of the voyage followed the news that Germany had surrendered. We were then off New Guinea. At sunset all who could, crowded the flight deck when every gun and thing that fired down to the Very pistols were let off in salvo after salvo. It was like a giant firework display. There was a short service of thanksgiving ending with the inevitable 'Abide with me' as the last colours of sunset faded over the mountains of New Guinea.

A week in Sydney meeting again friends made on the way up to the Pacific and then aboard a DC3 at Mascot, Sydney en route to Perth via Melbourne, Adelaide and Forest. A change of plane to a Quantas Airways Liberator to Exmouth Gulf and what was then the longest hop, to Ratmalana, Ceylon, which took fifteen hours. Finally an RAF Transport Command York from Ratmalana to Karachi, to Shaibah, Cairo, Malta and after nine days on the trip to touch down at Lyneham on 30th May. Home at last after sixteen months away. It looked good and it felt good if a little tinged with sadness.

HMS *Illustrious*.

CHAPTER THIRTEEN

The Last Lap

Soon after returning to the UK, I reported as required to Queen Anne's Mansions which housed the Department dealing with the postings of FAA aircrew. I met one of the officers in charge of postings whom I knew from former days. He said, 'Good God, where have you been? We have been looking all over the place for you. We had plans for you but you seemed to go missing and we couldn't find you.'

'Well,; I told him, 'I got bored with 845 Squadron in Ceylon and when David Foster came along with 849 Squadron in *Victorious*, I joined him and went off to the Pacific. We did clear it in Colombo.'

'Maybe,' he said with a smile, 'but you shouldn't have done it – we were wanting you here for other things. Still, you're here now thank God. You are going to be promoted to Lieutenant-Commander and given 711 Squadron at Crail in Scotland. Although the war is over in Europe, there is, as you know, a lot to do in the Far East and Pacific to lead up to the invasion of Japan. We want you to use your experience out there to train up the young Avenger pilots who will be going to the Far East at the end of their training. You'll be taking over from the present CO at the end of July but before you go to Crail we want you to do a lecture tour in Yorkshire. You see, the war is over in Europe as you know but we still have to keep up production of aircraft for the Jap war. The workers at the factories think that it's all over and are slackening off. We want you to go up there and tell them about the Pacific war and the importance of keeping up production till the Japs have been beaten. We'll give you details of all this as soon as possible – OK.'

I mumbled that command of 711 Squadron suited me fine but that I had never lectured in my life.

'Don't worry, just go along to the factories and shoot a whacking great line about dive bombing the Japs – they will love it.'

Eventually, instructions came through to report to the Hotel Victoria in Sheffield on the following Sunday evening. This I did and found a note there to tell me that I would be collected by a driver the following morning at 9 am. I had prepared some sort of speech dotted about with some horrendous stories of crashes, deaths and kamikazes and duly met my WAC driver next morning. Off we went to a local factory making aircraft components. I was met by the board of the company who told me about the work and personnel of the factory. What I was not prepared for was that I had to give the lecture in the canteen in the lunch hour. I was introduced by the manager and then the mike was handed over to me and I was on my own. I was quickly aware that I had to compete with the din of lunch in the huge canteen including the clatter of plates and cutlery. I never did quite know whether I came across – after all, Japan and the Pacific were a long way away and the war that these people knew about was over and peace was restored. How could I get over to them that there was an even bloodier war going on in the Pacific with big casualties in men and ships and planes with torture and murder thrown in for good measure. I think they were more interested in their steak and kidney pudding. Different factories but similar scenes followed during the week ending up with the biggest audience of all at the Blackburn Aircraft Works at Brough. A huge canteen with up to 2,000 people eating while I was talking. But by then, I had got my lecture to the stage where I didn't need notes and stories of the atrocities, bloodshed and horrific prangs rolled off the tongue to accompany their plum pudding. Whether anything I said had any effect on production was another matter – I doubt it.

Back home and then on to my posting to 711 Squadron at Crail in Fife, Scotland to take effect on 30th July. After the first flight in an Avenger since April, I was sent off to Hinstock in Shropshire to do an Instrument Flying course on the twin engine Oxford for a week. It was not a very memorable week either. I didn't take to the Oxford overmuch, nor to flying under a hood in cloud. I didn't think my instructors were very impressed by my blind flying as I was only given a 'C' rating. However, nothing depended on it and if nothing else, it was a new experience.

Back to Crail, but by then the Atom bombs had been dropped and the Japanese had surrendered. This meant the training of pilots for the Pacific was rather superfluous. Nevertheless, the training went on and I enjoyed teaching the youngsters the techniques of dive bombing in Avengers and close formation climbs hanging on to the prop to 13,000 feet. I must have been a devil for punishment as I also started flying the twin engine Anson, a slow, old but stable plane like a two engine Swordfish.

I certainly welcomed the move to a relatively peaceful backwater after four years in operational squadrons. There comes a time when the nerves need a rest from the incessant packing up and moving a complete squadron through to the hectic days of action filled with emotion-draining experiences. So I was glad of the more peaceful way of life that Crail and a training squadron had to offer. And I was delighted with the greater responsibility in being the CO of a squadron and the chance to pass on a little of my experience to the new boys. Rather them than me, I thought. There was, however, one aspect of the different life-style which I found difficult to meet. It can best be described in a word as atmosphere. For instance, while there was no lack of discipline in an operational squadron – far from it, as the fine tuning of operations, particularly from a carrier could not have been conducted without it. But somehow, it was self-imposed discipline due to the esprit de corps that existed and the determination on the part of everyone from top to bottom to help to achieve success. There was a pride in the squadron that no one was going to let down. Living conditions and such things as heat and long hours were accepted as part of the deal. There was a feeling of belonging to a team which was going to do better and look better than any other team. Those aspects of Naval or Fleet Air Arm life did not figure in the hum-drum of a training establishment like Crail. There, everything was ordered by the book. Service life was formal, correct and proper. Regulations were more important than atmosphere; administration and paper work tended to take over from a sense of achievement; the individual did not belong to a team, he was a cog in the formalities of an organization that had little personality. The transformation from the one to the other was not easy; at least, I didn't find it easy and as a result I became involved in two incidents because I did not obey the rules. Mea culpa.

The first occasion concerned a loyal and efficient petty officer in my squadron. One evening he had been involved in the movement of Avengers in one of the hangars. For some reason the wings of one of the planes were spread and one wing tip touched another plane causing a small amount of damage. Though it was irrelevant to the situation, the wing tips of the Avenger could be easily taken off and replaced. Nevertheless, damage had been done and the petty officer was in my report for next morning. I heard the witnesses and the officer in overall charge and after examining all the evidence, I decided there were extenuating circumstances and that a caution was the appropriate method of dealing with the charge. Next morning the phone rang and it was Commander (Flying) summoning me to the control tower. I hopped on my motor bike and made haste there, wondering what it was all about. The voice sounded like the prelude to a rocket, so I approached his office in a cautious way. And sure enough it was. Commander (Flying) had had a report on the petty officer charge and was not amused by my reaction to it. I was told that I should have put the petty officer in the Commander's report and he would have dealt with the offence appropriately. After tearing me off a strip, I was dismissed and told not to let it happen again but to obey the rules in future. However, we had a drink together in the mess that evening, so all was forgiven.

The second episode was rather more serious and a lack of judgement on my part born of a complete frustration with the system. It concerned the maintenance and servicing of aircraft. In first line squadrons, the ground crews of the squadron serviced their own planes whether ashore or afloat and they took pride in their work, knowing and working with aircrews who were flying the planes. By the time I got back to the UK, Royal Naval Air Stations had gone over to what was called central maintenance, that is, the servicing of all planes including squadron aircraft was undertaken by the station's central pool of fitters and riggers. In operational squadrons, servicing and maintenance was carried out extraordinarily quickly, often overnight in an emergency, so that the maximum number of planes was available at any given time. Central maintenance took much longer. I was annoyed at the apparently unnecessary delay as I had a lot of pupil pilots all needing as much flying as I could give them. And I made my views known to those in charge.

Now, Crail had a monthly news sheet. I was asked to contribute to it. Mistakenly, I thought this would be a good forum for airing my views on central maintenance. Commander (Flying) summoned me to his office again but this time, after giving me a rocket, he took me before the Captain of the Station. He took a very dim view and got exceedingly angry, suggesting that he might feel obliged to recommend that I leave the Navy. I thought to myself that that would really rather suit me to get back to civilian life but judged that I should keep my big mouth shut and not add petrol to an already roaring fire. I was pleased that when the time did come to leave, the captain gave me a good chit so perhaps all had again been forgiven. It taught me a lesson, however, that in some circumstances it is better to go through the back door rather than have a confrontation up front, especially where entrenched attitudes are involved. It also convinced me that I was not cut out for a career in the Navy. However, this feeling may well have been influenced by the fact that I was lucky enough to have another profession to go back to; I did in fact, the war apart, enjoy my five years in the Navy, five years that taught me a lot.

And so, just before Christmas and after many a party, I was demobilised and travelled back to Guildford and a legal career in London. I left the Navy with strangely conflicting emotions. Gone was the wonderful friendship, camaraderie, team spirit, constant help and cooperation from fellow officers and ratings alike, the *esprit de corps* of an operational squadron. Yes, one was alternately shit-scared or bloody bored but both were forgotten in the exhilaration of achievement and the companionship of friends. Now, it was all too obvious that one was on one's own. There was an atmosphere in peacetime and civilian life that every one was out for himself and to hell with anyone who got in the way.

'OK, pull up the ladder, Jack, I'm in board' was the general attitude. It was sad but true. However, the experience gained in the navy was to be of inestimable value and the many friends made during the many vicissitudes of the war were to be a great support in the years ahead. The fraternity of the flyer does not disintegrate however much you may have fought one another or on which side you might have been.

There is however one emotion, one experience that has remained above all others. It is that inexplicable, indescribable and very deep experience of flying. I have not known any flyer who doesn't admit to having been emotionally affected by the experience. It has something to do with the freedom of the air, of being away from the hustle and bustle, the pushing and shoving, the noise and tumult that exists on the ground. The flyer is alone, free, in control and at peace.

Receiving the DSC at Buckingham Palace (with the Authors's brother).

INDEX